A State of Independen is the problem and no. ... soiution

Mark Brolin

First published in the United Kingdom in 2016 by Endeavour Press Ltd.

Table of Contents

Foreword   5

Introduction   9

Chapter 1: A brief recapitulation of the EU history   15

Chapter 2: Dominating vested interests influencing the EU   37

Chapter 3: The six main reasons the EU will never fulfil its
promises   99

Chapter 4: Why staying within the EU is a recipe for a hazardous
political stalemate   118

Chapter 5: But the now inevitable EU downfall will be an
opportunity to start afresh   124

Chapter 6: Epilogue   137

Selected Bibliography   142

Endnotes   145

Foreword

The EU critique in this book is realist rather than idealist. History proves overwhelmingly that overreach is bound to follow any political camp – regardless of ideological belief system – if allowed to stay in power for a sufficiently long time. Why? Because given time any political establishment will, sooner or later, institutionalise its political friends more or less everywhere, including in the academic sphere. These friends will subsequently be consulted for 'expert' advice. Precisely as intended the decision making process will then be heavily skewed in favour of the political agenda of the paymasters. It will only be a question of time until politically convenient ideas transform into dogma which subsequent generations will be conditioned to believe. The operators of the political system, those actually holding power, will label opponents exercising little real power as dangerous subversives. As a consequence the establishment figures can and will perceive themselves as white knight saviours when centralising powers further. Increasingly they will also perceive it as nothing less than a moral duty to bully those who do not see the light - the critics - into silence. It is at this point political overshoot inevitably follows.

However, political instability will ensue due to a failure to deliver on the trio of grand political promises that typically surround every political mega project: peace, prosperity and domestic stability. Opinion makers will respond to turbulence by closing rank and solemnly attest that after much consideration they have concluded major change is imprudent during shaky times. Many voters will be swayed, if not by the glorious promises then by the authority of the backers: "If just about every professional testifies that the status quo alternative is the wisest and safest, how can it be otherwise?"

Historical evidence leaves no doubt this chain of events will pan out when a political group – any group – manages to gain a critical mass of power. Consequently it can be treated as a certainty, a sort of natural law of power politics.

For those willing to see it, Europe is yet again caught in precisely this kind of jumble. The main difference is that it takes place on a much grander scale than ever before. In line with the realist perspective of this book *every* idealist EU defence argument with the undertone of a mantra will be treated with scepticism. Why? Because as long as a political system actually does improve peace prospects, living standards and domestic political stability there will be little reason to play on the strings of idealism. Vague idealistic notions peddled in a biased way, such as the 'better-together' argument, are only truly needed when facts and numbers start to point downwards.

Of course the EU federalists are right when saying that all sorts of international co-operation can be beneficial. However, forced co-operation can also be the cause of friction whereas looser relationships can save strained relationships. Meaning that it will be nothing less than dangerous to apply the better-together argument as a *general* guiding principle. Doing so anyway amounts to emotional manipulation.

A similar logic applies to the EU federalist narrative surrounding the nation state. Of course the European nation state borders, which for decades have been much scorned by the EU federalists, were partly forged by paternalist rulers who also played shamelessly on emotional triggers. This still does not provide justification for doing the same thing on a bigger scale; least of all when the present European borders are at last undisputed by everyone but the federalists themselves.

Then again the book perspective would not be truly realist if not also acknowledging that idealistic touting is an integral part of the 'political show'. If a supranational entity works it works even if embedded in idealistic fluff. The author of this book, who has been privileged to live almost half his adult life in Sweden and the other half in the UK, was one of those who in 1994 voted for Sweden to join the EU while believing strongly in the value of the common market. Certainly, he was also naively believing in the solemn promises that the EU would not expand much further. Still, idealist scepticism has to cut both ways. Now when an alternative to sovereign European nation states is indeed on offer this alternative should not be criticised on the grounds of an *idealist* belief in nation state sovereignty. What really should matter is functional merit.

This book cleanses the EU debate from idealist ruffle of all sorts and then factually compares the functional merits of maintaining sovereign nation states with the functional merits of a supranational state.

A deliberate effort has been made to seek out facts and arguments presented not only by people typically promoted and praised by the establishment while serving a political purpose; but also the more independent minds who dare to challenge conventional thinking despite sometimes negative professional (and social) consequences.

Whether agreeing with the reasoning and conclusions in this book or not the reader will hopefully find it an honest and no nonsense attempt to cut beyond the political smokescreens that too often surround the EU debate.

No one but the author can assume responsibility for controversial viewpoints or lines of reasoning but a special thanks to those having provided valuable advice and encouragement ahead of publication, including Roland Vaubel, Professor of Economics at the University of Mannheim, Dr David Green, CEO Civitas, Philip Booth, The Institute of Economic Affairs, Professor William Shughart, J. Fish Smith Professor in Public Choice, Utah State University and Luke Johnson, Chairman of Risk Capital Partners, author, entrepreneur.

I dedicate this book to my one-of-a-kind wife. Without her patient support this book would not exist.

Introduction

Not since the democratic revolution has the parliamentary system changed as much as it has during the last decades of EU development. Even if not officially acknowledged it is certainly no exaggeration to talk about yet another parliamentary revolution. A big difference between the parliamentary revolution a hundred years ago, the *democratic* revolution, and the still ongoing parliamentary revolution, the *EU* revolution, is that the change back then was a great victory for those advocating stronger and closer links between the political establishment and the people. In that respect the EU revolution is a definite setback. Another big difference is that the democratic revolution was preceded by much discussion and executed with a big bang. The EU revolution has, notoriously, been orchestrated and executed much more quietly – even stealthily. Indeed, it is quite easy to describe the EU story since the early 1990s as a story of mission creep hidden behind a veil of diplomatic sophistication.

This is, actually, not particularly surprising. Why? Because it is the task of every politician and civil servant to promote his or her area of responsibility. In practice such promotion goes hand-in-hand with a continuous demand not only for an extended political mandate, but also budget increases. In one sense the inbuilt tendency to swell, that follows as a consequence, can be regarded as an expression of professional commitment. The fact that nobody within the public sector is risking personal money (only the money of the taxpayers), if things go sideways, certainly does nothing to moderate this tendency. Even the job risk is limited due to the strength of public sector employment protection. When the potential career upside is substantial and the potential downside minimal, who would not make the expansion demands?

Another characteristic of most large organisations (and private ones) is the creation of a glorifying self-image. This happens quite automatically as it is part of every job description to speak well of the organisation that pays the salary. Add the PR-and marketing professionals who, of course, are explicitly paid to boost the image. The fact that the official image of an organisation almost per definition is a public relations image – and therefore seductively distorted – does not prevent it from influencing the narrative within.

Combine the expansion bias of bureaucracy with the typically blown up self-image and you get an almost fool proof recipe for paternalism: "If people do not understand the need for expansion, then let's do it anyway. After all, we are on top of the power pyramid. Who has a better overview of what society needs? Now then, how can we roll things out without people overreacting?"

Certainly, there were *supposed* to be an effective stop gap. Member state public servants were *meant to* provide an effective counterweight to excessive EU demands. After all, if powers are transferred to the EU institutions, powers are simultaneously lost among national public servants. Quite effective, surely? Not really. Due to vested interests described in this book, far too many member state public servants have proven unwilling to offer much more than charade resistance.

Moreover, only in an ideal world does unchecked expansion bias stop when the original mission has been accomplished. In the real world, after the latter has happened, the goalposts are typically moved. Why? Because a growing bureaucracy will almost per definition gain more political clout and thereby a greater ability to push through further demands. There will never be a shortage of excuses: "Yes, yes, we said we should only deal with the common market but aren't labour market policies closely linked? How can you object, don't you care about the workers? And what about a common currency, a money matter is it not? But that must surely also mean fiscal responsibility? What then, about development aid? And human rights? How can you object, don't you care about those in trouble? Asylum policies, surely. Perhaps a European foreign policy co-ordinator? And now when we are already heavily involved in foreign policy, perhaps an army? Taxation rights? An anthem? A flag? By the way, national borders, aren't those a bit dated?"

It might feel tempting to dismiss the public servants who have orchestrated the 'expansion show' as simply hypocritical and deceitful. After all, they often passionately claim they care about open and honest debate as well as about democracy. Still many twist the narrative and are noticeably uninterested in consulting the people. However, it has to be kept in mind that the forces at work shaping internal opinion are so strong that an individual, arguably, does not stand a chance against 'the system'. It certainly does not help that human nature – we – are strongly inclined to persuade ourselves that we are doing the right thing even when we are not.

The human aspect has so far been sorely lacking from political science and in particular from any study of the European Union. The vast majority of EU books produced within the academic sphere assume, usually implicitly, that the public servants operating the system are logical, balanced and unselfish. Consequently every EU official will weigh serious critique as evenly as serious praise and seek neither more nor less powers than what has been determined through open rational dialogue. If someone, somehow, fails to do so technical safeguard procedures will kick in and make sure nothing happens which is out of place.

With this highly romantic take on public servants, skepticism towards the system will always be perceived as inappropriate[1]. If there is a problem, it will be due to some sort of accident or misunderstanding. The kneejerk reaction to problems is to simply table another meeting with the very same people as before and perhaps make some minor twists to the system. Possibly add another formal safeguard, for example yet another watchdog or another ombudsman. "Well, we'll make them independent of sorts but no need for total independence since everyone in our staff meet the highest standard and really can work things out between themselves. Sure, some voters still seem concerned. What about commissioning a number of academics to check the health of the system? Probably academics from those universities that just happen to be big EU grant recipients. No problem with that, we know these people and that makes the whole process a bit smoother. We are all professionals, right!"

However, books produced by academics (or other writers) who *are* part of the EU system – and an astonishingly large portion of EU book writers are – will more often than not be pointless, besides as propaganda tools. Which perfectly illustrates the point: it is only in a perfect (romantic) world people – we – are as professionally unbiased and rational as most of us think we are. In the real few people are unmoved by career interests, budget considerations, personal prestige, pressure groups, prejudices, (convenient) self-delusions, backroom dealing temptations as well as the fear-triggers commanded by people in authority even when at fault.

Indeed, irrationality and bias explain why operators within a political system will typically be adept at knocking around facts and arguments until the course of action that best serves personal career interests also just happens to seem like the most righteous one. Jonathan Haidt, one of the social and moral psychologists who is spearheading research around our political biases and prejudices, describes it as if we all possess an 'inner lawyer' rather than an inner judge or scientist[2]. He also argues that we use our reason not so much to shape our morals but to construct a defence for a course of action we have already arrived at instinctively. He moreover suggests that academics or people with a high IQ are often highly skilled at coming up with arguments; but only arguments defending already held positions, not the arguments of the opponents.

Haidt also explains why we tend to be so fiercely tribal in our logic. As long as opinions are possible to sync with the narrative of *our* tribe we allow deviations. Opinions beyond that are often met with insufferable intolerance and intimidation. Why? Because our flawed logic has assured us that 'the others' are so devilishly wrong that they are not worthy of the human respect we expect for ourselves.

This simultaneously explains why there really is plenty of good faith going around (in all political camps) and why leading public servants always seem able to find numerous motives for further expansion and, if necessary, also rule breaking: "If it is for a good cause, why then bother so much about the reasoning? If flawed, so be it as long as it advances our glorious mission."

Human nature has notoriously failed to sufficiently withstand the logic of Communist tyranny, Nazi dictatorship and theocratic despotism. Moreover, none of these systems would have survived even for a day unless thousands upon thousands of public servants had proven perfectly willing to 'do their duty'. Only to outsiders not reached by the PR-machinery was it obvious that the logic adopted was blatantly self-serving. How, then, can public servants be expected to resist the allures of a 'technocratic project' such as the EU?

All across Europe people are increasingly aware that the EU federalists have heavily overplayed their hand and thereby also severely diluted the healthy original core of the European project.[3] An even greater number of people are aware that the EU federalists have gone way beyond the democratic mandate granted by citizens across Europe.[4] Many are also well aware - or at least suspecting - that the public servants in the member states, those who were supposed to provide a counterweight, really have given the EU integrationists an easy ride.[5]

As a result there are now protest movements across Europe mirroring the present gulf between the political sphere and a sizeable group of people. It is of course not the first time in history a political elite stands fairly united against 'the people'[6]. Nor is it the first time a political elite simultaneously dismisses the people as being at fault. It is however the first time it has happened to such a stark degree during the democratic era.

The political game played out over recent years has many echoes in history. The newcomers on the political scene, the parties of discontent, have alleged that the incumbents are burying their heads in the sand. The incumbents have carried on as if every shred of critique has its origin among uninformed troublemakers - possibly racists - who fail to understand 'the vision'. Dogmatism on both sides have strengthened already prevailing biases even further and thereby widened the rift. Soon arguments that perhaps started only as PR-slogans became widely believed among activists in both camps. This includes the belief in a story which has always been a hallmark of fierce political battles: only opponents are driven by self-interest whereas sympathisers are primarily driven by concerns about society. Such hero-versus-villain dramaturgy is surprisingly effective even today.[7] One major reason is that it generates a lot more positive excitement and attention than a more level-headed analysis, both among friendly media outlets and among the rank and file party members that tend to decide the leadership contests of every party. Somewhat ironically this means that as the quality of the debate has deteriorated, the number of people acting in good faith might have actually increased.

These are the main reasons most political camps are simultaneously adamant they are occupying the moral high ground. Perhaps no other perception has done more to deepen the animosity between 'EU apologists' and 'EU thrashers'. However, there is good reason to believe that the majority of the people are neither; many people simply want a European project in the common market shape it was once intended to be. This is a book making the case for precisely such a direction while also making clear that the only way to fulfil such a desire it is to abandon the current experiment, the EU, and start afresh.

It is also a book that can be regarded as a call to arms against political romanticism. Never in the history of politics have romantic preconceptions led to romantic outcomes. Quite the contrary. Chapter one offers a recapitulation of the EU history while highlighting how one expansion of EU power has always led to another. Chapter two portrays, while applying a markedly realist perspective, what really motivates the movers and shakers within the EU system. Chapter three describes why hell will freeze over before the EU manages to fulfil its promises of economic prosperity and enhanced peace prospects. Chapter four describes why the window of corrective change has already closed and why staying within the EU will be equivalent to underwriting a perpetual state of political stalemate and economic limbo. Chapter five summarises why trading will carry on quite unhampered, after a Brexit, after the dust has settled, and why it will benefit both future growth and security prospects. Chapter five moreover makes the case for establishing 'EC II' as well as for basing additional international co-operation on the principle of functional and organisational separation. Such a principle, if upheld, makes sure that one supranational entity will never again become so strong that it manages to make nonsense of the public debate and thereby of democracy itself. Chapter six summarises the key findings.

Chapter 1: A brief recapitulation of the EU history

The EU story began in 1952 when six countries – West Germany, France, Belgium, Netherlands, Luxembourg and Italy – founded the European Coal and Steel Community (ECSC). As the name implies, the aim of the ECSC was to ensure that coal and steel were traded and shipped duty-free between the member states. Economics were linked with the ambition to maintain peace: better to trade with each other than to shoot at each other. In addition, control of coal and steel production in the French-German border region (Ruhr and Saar) had played a decisive role in the run-up to both world wars. Allowing these commodities, central to military strength, to move duty-free across borders, would reduce the risk of a country mustering such comparative material advantage that the temptation to go to war would again be irresistible.

Just a few years later, in 1957, the Treaty of Rome established the European Economic Community expanding the Customs Union to more products (but no more countries).

In order to extend the customs union to agriculture, the EEC had to effectively copy the generous agricultural subsidies and high external trade tariffs which the French government up to that point had employed to protect French farmers.[8] In practice, this agreement meant that West Germany, a buffer state during the Cold War, paid a price to establish closer ties with an ally central for both economic strength and security. To Germany the European project also had the added benefit that it helped pave the way for treatment as an equal rather than a pariah on the international scene.[9]

The Treaty of Rome moreover included two provisions that would prove essential for *later* developments: a commitment to "ever closer union amongst the peoples of Europe" and the "four freedoms", commitment to the free movement of goods, workers, services and capital. Back then, however, few politicians treated these two provisions as much more than nice rhetoric ornaments.

The six founding members also established the European nuclear energy cooperation (Euratom) in 1958. Its then rather uncontroversial aim was to promote the new and hyper-trendy nuclear energy industry.

In 1967 the European Coal and Steel Community, the European Economic Community and Euratom came together under one umbrella. As a result the European Community (EC) was born.

It would take another several decades before the EC expanded its *content*, but *institutionally* European cooperation now began to take a form which is similar to that of today. With the birth of the EC, the Commission was established as a common executive body for all three organisations. The three largest member states (West Germany, France and Italy) had two representatives on the Commission, the other countries one each.

Already in 1958 a common advisory assembly had been established, the Joint Assembly, which was renamed the European Parliament in 1962 and was meant to be the democratic check on EC decisions. The parliamentarians were initially nominated by their national parliaments, and lacked formal powers. This changed during the 1970s. In two stages, in 1970 and 1975, the European Parliament was given a formal voice in the Commission's budget. In this way, the parliament ceased to be *merely* a talking shop. In 1979 popular elections to the European Parliament were held for the first time.

Even a joint council of ministers has a history stretching back to 1967. Admittedly, the EC's operational goals were then so very clearly restricted to trade and industry that a long period of time could pass between ministerial meetings. As long as the majority of issues were of a rather uncontroversial technical trade (and less political) nature, there was quite simply no need to meet regularly in order to reach decisions at ministerial level. Still, everyone knew that no important decisions could be pushed through without the Council's approval. Just as today, it was the nature of the issue discussed that determined which group of member state ministers met. Meetings between prime ministers, finance ministers and foreign ministers were seen as particularly important.

During this period, there were *attempts* at deepening the integration amongst the six states. Giving more powers to the Community would have required treaty change and Charles de Gaulle, French President from 1959 to 1969, ensured that all attempts to do so failed miserably.

He fiercely opposed all moves towards more supranational decision-making while fearing that France's influence would be reduced. It certainly also mattered that De.Gaulle simultaneously was presiding over the winding up of the French colonial empire[10]. Giving up even more national sovereignty was not seen as politically feasible, especially not to an institution that included the old German archenemy. This did not hinder German 'federalist' Walter Hallstein, EC President from 1958 to 1967, to have a go. In 1965 Hallstein proposed to give the EC the right to impose customs duties. He also proposed a system of majority voting which would have abolished the decision vetoes that France and other member states could in practice exercise at will. The French turned out to be isolated in opposition whereas Hallstein enjoyed considerable support both in his home country and from the other EC commissioners. Even if Hallstein may have thought that he, as a consequence, struck from a position of strength, he ran straight into the full force of Gaullism. The French President withdrew all French representatives from the EC, both at Commissioner level and official level. This crisis, 'the empty chair crisis', lasted for seven months and punctured Hallstein's plan for the foreseeable future. Hallstein himself failed to gain renewed support when his mandate ran out.

In some ways, this crisis constituted the peak of French influence over the European Project.

Disputes that *could* be resolved were often of a more limited trade technical nature. As a last resort, these disputes were determined by the *Court of Justice of the European Communities* which had been formed under a different name as early as 1952. The Court would prove hugely important in driving European integration (see below).

This means that there were, in 1967, four de facto EC institutions: the Commission, the Parliament, the European Court and the Council of Ministers (even if the latter was yet to be formalised). In 1970 the three EC bodies established a common auditing unit. Its task was to scrutinise the use of the EC budget. Eventually, this auditing unit was renamed the European Court of Auditors.

In 1973 Britain, Ireland and Denmark entered the EC. This was the first time the number of members was extended, the first "enlargement" if you will. All three new member countries had applied for membership, while hoping to improve economic growth and reduce unemployment and simultaneously evade economic and political marginalisation. Britain had applied for EC membership as early as 1963 but had been blocked by, not totally surprisingly, General de Gaulle. His fear that time was that Britain would act as a Trojan Horse for American interests, whilst also watering down the EC's protectionist agricultural policy. This is one way he, in the 1965 presidential campaign, defended his stance: "Of course one can jump up and down yelling Europe! Europe! Europe! But it amounts to nothing and it means nothing."

A mix of economic and security motivations also lay behind the accession of the former military dictatorships Greece (1981), Spain (1986) and Portugal (1996). The primary geopolitical motivation for these countries had less to do with the Cold War and more with threats to *domestic political* security. By establishing ties with more stable democracies, and a rules-based trading zone, economic growth would be promoted and the risk of lapsing back into dictatorship reduced.

The Single European Act, a milestone in the European project, came into force in 1987. The aim of the act was to realise the "the four freedoms" promised in the Treaty of Rome. To avoid individual member states constantly blocking unpopular moves to open up domestic markets, the SEA included a rather radical reform to the voting system: requirement for unanimity was dropped in a number of areas, replaced by so-called qualified majority voting (QMV). From now on, only a certain number of countries – using a system of weighted votes - had to agree for a proposal to pass in areas relating to the single market. Even if the veto right were kept in relation to some areas, notably employment law, the SEA was nothing short of a quantum leap for the Single Market.

It was also the SEA that formalised the Council of Ministers. From now on meetings were taking place at regular intervals rather than on an ad hoc basis.

Even though the SEA bore clear liberal fingerprints, France was still in the driving seat, but now pushing for *deeper* integration. The dust had somewhat settled after the dismantling of the colonial empire. This meant that international outreach was once again politically feasible. Most importantly, now when the empire was gone the country's elite had spotted an opportunity to *use the European project* to multiply French influence on the international stage.

Those prospects improved considerably when the French President François Mitterrand (President from 1981 to 1995) managed to place one of his own men, Jacques Delors (a former Finance Minister), as President of the Commission (from 1985 to 1995). Mitterrand and Delors, both socialists, joined forces in trying to develop a European Community that intervened more actively in an increasing number of areas, while simultaneously siding more with the trading unions and employees over businesses.

Under normal circumstances this ambition would probably have been halted – or moderated – by Germany where the right-winger Helmut Kohl (Christian Democrat) was Chancellor (1982–1998). However, the fall of communism and disintegration of East Germany meant that the circumstances were far from normal. In fact, times were absolutely extraordinary. Mitterand, like Thatcher, genuinely feared a united and resurgent Germany.

This triggered a stand-off – and compromise - between Mitterand, Kohl and Thatcher, three exceptionally strong political figures. The stand-off between Mitterand and Kohl would change the nature of European integration. Playing the World War II guilt card, Mitterand – like his predecessors – was determined to make Germany pay a price for the country's full re-integration into Europe. In exchange for France's tacit approval for the reunification of East and West Germany, Helmut Kohl gave in to two French demands: the so-called Social Chapter (adopted in 1989), a first set of EC labour market regulations and secondly, a single currency for the EC.

Now it was the UK's Margaret Thatcher who offered the stoutest resistance. Just like Charles de Gaulle a couple of decades earlier, Thatcher would have none of it. Even at the beginning of her term in office, Thatcher had fiercely negotiated a reduction in the UK's net contribution to the EC's common budget, arguing that that UK got a horrible deal, particularly with respect to farm subsidies. Thatcher famously exclaimed "I want my money back." After tough negotiations, Thatcher won what according to EU jargon is a 'rebate', a term implying that the people in Brussels were generous. The rebate is now the very symbol of British resistance to European integration – its hand-bag euroscepticim. Curiously, it also built in permanent tension between

France and the UK in EU budget talks. Due to the way it is structured, France is always paying the most towards the UK's rebate.

Jacques Delors quickly understood there was no point in trying to sway Margaret Thatcher - the lady was not for turning. Instead he zoomed in on the British workers' movement and the Labour Party, which during the 1980s had been strongly sceptical about the European 'free trade' project. In a speech to the British *Trades Union Congress* in 1988, Delors declared that the EC would guarantee high levels of workers' protection. Some days later, Thatcher retorted, "We have not successfully rolled back the frontiers of the state in Britain, only to see them reimposed at a European level, with a European Super state exercising a new dominance from Brussels."

The deadlock resulted in a political compromise. With Germany watching from the side-lines, Delors pushed through his labour market agenda, buying off the British with an "opt out" from the Social Chapter, promised in the next Treaty. British labour legislation would not be subordinated to EC labour law.

That opt-out, however, was severely undermined before it entered into force when the Commission proposed the infamous Working Time Directive – regulating working hours and conditions. The Commission declared the WTD to be a "health and safety" matter advancing the single market. "A practical contribution towards creating the social dimension of the internal market", as the Commission put it.

The move was as clever as it was cheeky. Unlike labour policy, health and safety was subject to qualified majority meaning that the UK suddenly lacked a veto over the proposal. Britain was outvoted and had to accept the WTD despite its opt-out. A furious John Major sued the Commission at the European Court of Justice. However, the ECJ, bound by the EU treaties to practice "sincere and mutual cooperation" with the other EU institutions, ruled in favour of the Commission. Britain's Tory party has never forgiven what is considered a clear sleight of hand by Brussels. The ECJ has since extended the scope of the WTD on at least eight occasions. Margaret Thatcher would later conclude that the powers that the Single European Act granted Brussels were "abused in order to push corporatist and collectivist legislation upon Britain by the back door"[11].

This episode illustrates the important role that the ECJ had come to play for European integration, a role it had continued to play up until this day. Already in 1979, the ECJ had precipitated the SEA by ruling in favour of "mutual recognition" of goods, meaning member states had to recognise each other's standards (in the famous Cassis de Dijon ruling). It was a huge step forward for cross-border trade.

A bit over a decade later, the Court introduced a new concept - "EU citizens" – ruling that they can move to and settle in any member states, and enjoy certain rights, even if unemployed. This extended free movement from "workers" to "people" – a change that explains much of the heated debate around free movement that has captured so many headlines in the 2010s.

The ECJ has moreover invented various doctrines, for example, the doctrine of the primacy of EU law (EU law prevails when there is conflict between European law and the law of Member States) and the so-called direct-effects doctrine (EU law can take direct effect in member states, meaning that national courts must uphold certain laws even if not ratified in the national parliaments). This assigns more political powers to the European Union despite no basis for such doctrines in the European treaties.[12]

The added labour market interventions helped Delors in his quest to win over Labour. In part owing to Tory splits over Europe, Labour leader Tony Blair won a landslide victory in the 1997 election. At this stage it was confirmed that Labour had developed a considerably more positive attitude to the EU. One of Tony Blair's first acts as Prime Minister was to remove the UK's opt out from the EU Social Chapter.

Social policy notwithstanding, Delors had the final word over Thatcher in an even more significant area: the single currency. In 1990, Margaret Thatcher was deposed in a palace coup, which primarily had its origins in her resistance to the euro's forerunner. Two of her previously closest government confidants, Nigel Lawson and Geoffrey Howe, insisted on pegging the pound to the Exchange Rate Mechanism (ERM), a preparatory stage to the euro project. The experiment turned out to be a complete failure. In September 1992, very unwillingly and during great market drama, the UK was forced to abandon the ERM.

The ERM fiasco left some scars in the UK but, under French auspices, there was nothing stopping the euro project itself from going ahead.

Viewed from Paris, the euro was designed to permanently tie Germany to a Gaullist Europe, not least by reducing the dominance of the German Bundesbank – which had emerged as one of Europe's most powerful and credible economic forces. As Delors famously put it, "Not all Germans believe in God, but all Germans believe in the Bundesbank."

In others words, the euro project was conceived in power politics - not economics. For this to work, however, the French needed a new, grand Treaty.

The 1991 Maastricht Treaty, ratified in 1993, gave birth to the EU and laid the groundwork for the euro. Three pillars together made up the EU. The first pillar, still named the EC, contained the original three bodies (the ECSC, Euratom and the EEC, i.e. the single market). The second pillar contained foreign and military policy while the third pillar contained police and judicial co-operation. The second and third pillars were still primarily subject to so-called 'inter-governmental' decision-making – national leaders were calling the shots with limited input by the Brussels institutions.

The euro only began to replace national currencies in 1999, but Maastricht created its basic structure and rules. Most importantly, the European Monetary Institute (EMI), overtaken in 1998 by the European Central Bank. The one and only aim of the ECB was to safeguard price stability in the eurozone. To ensure fiscal discipline and a stable euro once it was launched, the Treaty also established the famous "Maastricht criteria". At least in theory these were meant to put limits on how much money governments in the EU could spend, a country's deficit – the difference between expenditure and income - could not exceed 3 per cent while total debt would have to be less than 60 per cent of the size of the country's economy. It was not entirely clear why EU leaders agreed on these particular limits, but they did.

To calm German anxiety about giving up the beloved D-Mark, a central tenet of the country's post-World War II economic miracle, the Treaty also instituted a "no bailout principle". No eurozone country was ever going to be forced to bail out another.

Taken together, Maastricht, massively expanded the EU's powers, directly and indirectly. Looking back, the Treaty and its commitment to a common currency did three things: it turned the EC into a fundamentally political project; it put Britain on a permanent coalition course with

France and Germany; and – ironically - contrary to Mitterand's strategic gamble, it planted the seeds for again making Germany Europe's most powerful country.

It was no co-incidence that it was Delors rather than Hallstein that went down in history as the figure who in earnest launched the European federal project. As long as the Cold War raged, with missiles pointing in all kinds of directions and spies feared to be lurking in every corner, pooling of national sovereignty was limited by serious trust issues. In addition, a too overtly political EU would probably have upset the balance of power between East and West, risking a Soviet backlash. Up until 1989, therefore, the European Project had some clear geopolitical limitations, in terms of both geography and policy.

However, with the Iron Curtain torn to pieces, the coast was clear for the EU integrationists. The Maastricht Treaty was rapidly followed by the Amsterdam Treaty in 1997 and the Nice Treaty in 2001 – both transferring a batch of new powers from national capitals to Brussels.

As it turns out, however, it was not only the Soviet Union that had offered resistance to further EU integration. Though some may have considered the Maastricht Treaty and the launch of a single currency a no-brainer – 'how can you have a single market without a single currency?' – to the EU elite's surprise, the citizens across Europe didn't all agree.

This spectacularly included the Danes. In a referendum in 1992, a majority of Danish voters said No to the Maastricht Treaty. A commitment to the euro and various other measures proved to be steps too far. There was great irritation in Brussels. This would not do at all. Special negotiations with Denmark followed, which produced the 'Edinburgh agreement', an agreement designed to appease the annoying Danes. Following awkward negotiations Denmark was given opt-outs from the euro, and special arrangements in relation to defence, police and crime law.[13] In a new referendum in May 1993 the Danes voted yes. The Maastricht Treaty was ratified and entered into force the very same year.

Despite this historic victory the federalists had not had enough and knew how to play it in order to open new treaty negotiations. Delors and other prominent EU figures talked openly about even deeper integration but did simultaneously swear allegiance to the so-called subsidiarity principle, which first was mentioned in the Maastricht Treaty. This is a principle that at least in theory means that the EU should only make decisions if it is clear – beyond all reasonable doubt – that the area in question cannot be handled better by national or local politicians (or better, individuals and families). The subsidiarity principle was said to guarantee that further economic and political integration cooperation would not happen unless there were *really* good reasons behind it. This guarantee was also in part aimed at many doubters in Sweden, Finland and Austria, countries which were applying for membership in the mid-1990s.

The balancing act was masterly. Sweden, Finland and Austria all voted 'the right way', and joined in 1995. The European project then had 15 members. Citizens in other places were still not convinced, however. In separate referendums Norway and Switzerland voted 'the wrong way' on a few occasions, but the Brussels elite saw them as anomalies. One had oil, the other was a niche economy with a unique (and far too democratic) political system. Up to this day, Brussels diplomats still speak about the "Swiss accident."

Not least by half promising to regulate the only vague wording concerning the subsidiarity principle, a vagueness that had been heavily criticised, the EU federalists also managed to open new treaty negotiations.

With the 1997 Amsterdam Treaty, which came into force in 1999, political power was for the first time expressly transferred to the EU institutions. This included amongst other some decisions related to asylum and immigration policy. Schengen, the European passport agreement which had been concluded in 1985, but then left outside the EC because of deviating opinions among member states, was now also integrated within the EU.[14] As before, there were plenty of helpful and typical explanations as to why a new treaty was needed: 'These changes are quite natural if we want to get Schengen to work? Also, it is much easier to cooperate if everything is in one place.'

Even more areas moved from unanimity to majority voting. In this way, it became more difficult for individual member states to kick up a fuss. The European Parliament also strengthened its power significantly since the number of areas decided by so-called co-decision – both the Council of Ministers and MEPs have to agree before a proposal can become law – was extended significantly. Taken together this meant that even more areas were decided at the EU level with less ability for democratically elected national politicians to block them. Was that really consistent with the subsidiarity principle? 'Well, hold your horses, *all* areas were not affected, only, for example, monetary policy, the environment, public health, consumer protection, right of establishment, transports, regional support, equality of opportunity and development aid. In any case the economy is booming. Doesn't this show the superior value of European integration?'

Still, referendums were needed once again, this time in Denmark and Ireland. The reason is that both in Denmark and Ireland the constitution requires a referendum if decisions are considered to affect the constitution. The supposed only way to get around that is if 5/6 of the members of parliament support the amendment.

To avoid the turbulence from the last time referendums were held but Denmark, Ireland and also Britain were granted exceptions already in advance. These exceptions applied to the Schengen rules as well as asylum and immigration policy. That did the trick. Both the people of Denmark and Ireland voted yes. Did this mean that the EU integrationists were at last happy?

'Well, we can't be quite satisfied. It is true that the subsidiary principle we value so highly is something we didn't get the opportunity to really tackle this time either. We must start working on a new treaty!'

The Nice Treaty was signed in 2001 and came into force in 2003. One of its main aims was to prepare for the great geographical enlargement of the EU which took place in 2004. A major headache was how weighted voting would work after the accession of numerous small member states. The big countries demanded extra votes because of their larger populations. They were also eager to make sure that small states could not gang up to outmanoeuvre much larger states like Germany. The result was, and could only be, a political compromise[15].

With the Nice treaty, the number of areas that only required a qualified majority for decision making was also extended further. In addition, even more areas that governments had previously sorted out between themselves were moved into the first pillar, including copyright issues and industrial rights. 'Why not bring everything into the first pillar? Much easier to coordinate if everything is in one place!' With the Nice Treaty the EU was also, for the first time, assuming responsibilities touching on military matters; The Western European Union (WEU) – a European defence association and a form of relic from the Cold War – was incorporated into the EU structure.

All of these continued 'simplifications' of the decision-making process were said to be necessary in order to ensure that the EU would run smoothly after enlargement.

Ireland's government, unlike Denmark's, made the assessment that the Nice Treaty affected its own constitution. Thereby another referendum was required. The Irish political establishment supported the Treaty so the Yes vote was expected to be a pure formality. That expectation was wrong. A majority of Irish voted No. This time the concern was primarily about the EU's military plans. The EU phrasing was vague. Would the EU be able to force Ireland to send its sons and daughters to war?

Renegotiations followed resulting in the 'Seville Declaration': the EU assured Dublin that Irish soldiers could not be sent to war zones without the approval of the UN, the Irish government and the Irish Parliament. The declaration did not have any binding legal status, but that 'detail' was not given much attention during the "Nice II" referendum campaign. The second time the Irish people 'came to their senses' which meant that they voted Yes to the Treaty. At last green light also for Nice.

'Then again, subsidiarity is really important. A crucial challenge which still hasn't been tackled satisfactorily. And we do consider it really important. We immediately need to start working on another reform treaty!'

At this point, it was becoming clear that the citizens across the member states, still 15, were not entirely on board. In the 2001 Laeken Declaration by EU leaders admitted that "European institutions must be brought closer to its citizens... Many also feel that the Union should involve itself more with their particular concerns, instead of intervening, in every detail, in matters that by their nature better left to Member States' and regions' elected representatives."

The Declaration also explicitly stated that the EU should consider "restoring tasks to the member states." A process was initiated – the European Convention – that was meant to reconsider the EU's priorities and produce a new "reform treaty". However, despite the promising start, the process was yet again almost completely hijacked by integrationists.

Charged with heading up the convention was arch-federalist and former French President Valéry Giscard d'Estaing.

The game was over before it even started. Far from a "reform treaty" devolving powers to citizens, in 2003, Giscard d'Estaing presented a draft constitution that moved in exactly the opposite direction. The very terms constitution signals an ambition to move from cooperation to a state.[16] He proudly exclaimed: "We have sown a seed... Instead of a half-formed Europe, we have a Europe with a legal entity, with a single currency, common justice, a Europe which is about to have its own defence."

According to the draft proposal, the pillar system would be scrapped and along with it all remaining international (multilateral) elements in the EU. *Everything* that came under the second and third pillars would be transferred to the first pillar.

The EU spokespersons claimed on the one hand that the consequences were enormous and on the other that they were close to insignificant. 'We do so much already, what does it matter if we do a bit more? Simplification, coordination, uniformity. Who could disagree, the economy is doing so well! Take note also that this is a unique opportunity to develop the EU into a world player on the big stage, a counterweight to the USA, Russia and China, simply a guarantor for peace!'

In 2004, the Heads of Government (or Heads of State) of *all* European member states, by then 25, signed the treaty. However, to become law, it required the democratic approval in all member states.

Referendums in Denmark and Ireland were unavoidable despite EU leader attempts to tone down the practical impact of the treaty. This time other countries, even though not required by their constitutions, had caught on as well. 'Why shouldn't we get to vote if the Danes and the Irish do?' In the end, eight countries opted for referendums. Four of these were carried out. In Spain and Luxembourg the yes side won easily. However, then a shock followed. A majority of voters in both France and the Netherlands – two EU founding members – voted No. The other planned referendums, including that in the UK, were called off. The British referendum would almost certainly have generated a No vote, which in turn might have halted European integration indefinitely.

Stunned EU leaders called for a "period of reflection." What to do now? After three years of careful deliberation the answer was obvious: try again.

A new treaty was formulated, the Lisbon Treaty. The sensitive term 'constitution' was removed as were references to a common flag and common national anthem. The Brits received some further reassurances on judicial cooperation. The format for the new document was a virtually unreadable "amending Treaty". Besides these changes it is difficult to distinguish the differences between the draft constitution and the Lisbon Treaty.

In Giscard d'Estaing's words: "Public opinion will be led to adopt, without knowing it, the proposals that we dare not to present to them directly…all the earlier proposals will be in the new text, but will be hidden and disguised in some way."

The Lisbon Treaty scrapped the pillar structure. Foreign and security policy as well as cooperation on police and crime issues were now all subject in some way to the Commission and European Parliament.

The EU was also given its own juridical person. This means that in exactly same way as an ordinary state, the EU can enter into treaties with external states.

A new three-way system of powers was also introduced, which gave the EU either exclusive powers, shared powers with the member states, or supporting powers. For example, the EU was given exclusive decision-making powers over large parts of economic policy, in particular for the eurozone states. Shared competence meant a joint right for EU and the member states to make decisions, but member states can legislate in this area *only if the EU has not already done so*. Notably, the Lisbon treaty stipulates that this competence applies to "the area of freedom, security and justice", an area created after the cooperation on police and crime matters was merged with asylum and refugee policy. Environment, energy, transport, social policy and consumer protection are other areas of shared responsibility. Supporting competence, involving areas such as human health, education and culture, means that the EU does not have the right to override the EU member states but still get involved.

The idea was to clarify the division of powers between the EU and member states. In reality it made the division more blurred than ever.

Chairmanship of the European Council ceased to rotate between the member state heads of state or heads of government. That role was instead taken over by a permanent President. Also the chair of the council for foreign affairs ceased to rotate; from now on it automatically ended up with the EU's own High Representative of the Union for Foreign Affairs, originally called EU Foreign Minister – a term that was dropped because it was considered too controversial. The Treaty also introduced the establishment of a new body, the European External Action Service, which has quite a few attributes of a "foreign ministry."

Perhaps the most important change in the Lisbon Treaty was the strengthened role of the European Parliament. The new treaty means that the European Parliament (EP) decides jointly with national ministers – via co-decision - in 90 per cent of all EU decisions (now known as the ordinary legislative procedure). Lisbon also gave the EP an effective veto over trade deals the EU strikes with the rest of the world, and an important role in deciding the European Commission President. The idea was to "transfer democracy" to the EU, however, in retrospect it is questionable whether giving more powers to the EP has done much to reconnect the EU with citizens.

The Lisbon Treaty also gives the ECB an official status as an institution. In this way, finally the EU today has seven institutions: the European Commission, the European Parliament, the European Council, the Council of the European Union, the European Court of Auditors, the Court of Justice of the European Union and the European Central Bank.

Through the so-called 'passerelle clauses' the Lisbon Treaty also makes some possible future treaty reforms easier. The term passerelle refers to the French word for a footbridge, which is supposed to signal a temporary nature. However, crucially, no end date is given. There are various passerelle clauses in the Treaty, which effectively allows for EU policy areas to move from unanimity to QMV without a Treaty change. This can happen if all member state governments agree to the change, no referendums required.

There was also a second invention, the ability to pursue so-called "limited" treaty change – altering some parts of the EU treaties without necessarily changing anything "fundamental".

Such innovations are, yet again, diplomatic masterstrokes. In practice the EU leaders again allowed themselves a broader scope to press ahead with more integration without necessarily triggering referendums and thereby an uncertain people's consultation. Since the Lisbon Treaty, EU leaders have used the limited treaty change mechanism in order to allow for a eurozone "bailout fund".

At long last the application of the subsidiarity principle was regulated. National parliaments were given the chance to object to a proposed EU law. That was, at least, a formal victory of sorts for those objecting to further integration. However, in practice the subsidiarity mechanism remains weak. Current rules require a third of member states' national parliaments to protest against a European Commission proposal when referring to the subsidiarity principle. It has to happen within eight weeks of the proposal being tabled. This means national MPs might need to put most other things aside in order to digest and discuss the often lengthy Commission proposals – and thereafter synchronize with MPs of other member states. Even if the required number of national parliaments do present a formal protest, the Commission will only have to *review* its proposal. It is not *obligated* to revise or withdraw it. This means that the national parliaments, ultimately, have to rely on the Commission's goodwill. This isn't always forthcoming. In 2013, eleven national parliaments objected to a Commission proposal for a European Public Prosecutor. The Commission has since decided to press ahead with the plan anyway.

So the Lisbon Treaty extended the EU's powers further with still very limited democratic counter-checks.

There were plenty of resistance to the Treaty. The Danes considered a referendum until the last minute, but the political elite got away with claiming it didn't change the constitution (resulting in a Court case). Poland's government objected to losing relative weight in future voting rules. Britain was apprehensive because the charter of fundamental rights could create "new rights" in the UK. The UK's Conservative opposition also claimed that the Labour government had deceived the people by dropping a previous referendum pledge, despite the Constitution and Lisbon Treaty being near identical. The government of the Czech Republic expressed concern because the descendants of the Sudeten Germans would be able to lay claim to assets that had changed hands after the Second World War. Special opt-outs and arrangements were allowed for all these countries, but no referendums.

Only Ireland did hold a referendum. The pattern now had an almost ritual character. The people voted no on the first occasion. Renegotiations followed. The key Irish concern this time was whether the charter of human rights infringed on Catholic Ireland's legislation on "value issues" such as abortion, homosexuality and euthanasia. Ireland was given another legally non-binding protocol and a promise it would keep its Commissioner in future. After having given the wrong answer the first time around, when asked again, the Irish voted the right way. It certainly played into the hands of the EU integrationists that, by then, Ireland's real estate price bubble had burst and the economy was in freefall. The Yes campaigners presented constant warnings about losing out on foreign investment and marginalisation if voting No. Perhaps, more than anything else, the Irish public, still sceptical about the merits of the Treaty, was scared into voting 'Yes'.

Out of the fire into the frying pan. Just as the Lisbon Treaty finally came into force, ending what some described as a "constitutional crisis", Europe's real crisis hit.

By spring 2010, the eurozone crisis cast a long shadow over Europe. It would take almost three years before the immediate existential threat to the euro subsided – and then only temporarily.

The greatest headache was based on Greece having cooked its books. Goldman Sachs had been brought in to help make Greece's debt look "presentable" and meet the Maastricht criteria. Deal done, but many remained suspicious. As former Trade Commissioner Karel de Gucht put it, "We knew that Greece was cheating, it was clear as soon as they joined that there was something wrong [with their figures]".

However, a long line of federalists asserted that a small country, which only accounted for 2.5 per cent of the eurozone GDP, could do little harm. There was also a tactical consideration openly admitted by the former European Commission president Romano Prodi put it, "When the euro was born everyone knew that sooner or later a crisis would occur... that would force joint co-ordination of fiscal policies."

In December 2010, the then newly elected Greek government revealed the country's debt to GDP was almost 150 per cent, not 90 per cent as previously thought, and certainly not anywhere near the Maastricht criteria. So, did that mean they were kicked out? After all, if Greece was not fulfilling the criteria and these criteria were considered important would that not be the best thing to do keep the Euro healthy and the Greek economy able to yet again leverage its previous low cost advantage?

Well, that would have reversed the centralisation agenda and was certainly not the line of reasoning adopted by the EU integrationists. Instead they started claiming that the crisis illustrated that there was an inbuilt need for even more fiscal centralisation. Some even started to use the argument that was used against them when the euro project was first designed: "How can you have a currency union without a fiscal union?"

This was the start of the carpet-bombing of macroeconomic centralisation initiatives that followed (more about these later).

Greece, Ireland, Portugal, Cyprus and (in a limited way) Spain have all been forced to seek bailouts from the EU, shedding to pieces the Maastricht Treaty's no bailout clause and thereby smashing a promise made to the Germans in the 1990s. The ECB has bought sovereign bonds, effectively financing governments, despite its own mandate expressively forbidding state financing (another promise to the Germans).

The European Commission has been given more powers to supervise countries' economies, and in an attempt to uphold the Maastricht criteria, the right to "reject" member states budgets if considered too wasteful.

The EU has established a "Banking Union", with the ECB at the centre and tasked with supervising the eurozone's 6,000 banks. This structure even includes a eurozone financial backstop for banks that go bust – a de facto guarantee to prop them up in case of emergencies. This would have been unthinkable only a few years ago.

Far from its original mandate defined in the 1990s, the ECB is now in charge of setting interest rates, supervising banks and, in effect, underwriting both government finances and banks.

What is more, the eurozone crisis has also been used by the EU federalists to start suggesting powers of taxation, most controversially a financial transaction tax. The fact that such powers are not regulated in any of the treaties is obviously treated as a de facto go ahead.

So then, did all the centralisation measures, allegedly with the purpose of stabilising the Euro, help? Arguably they have been strongly contra productive while making it possible for Greece to accumulate an even higher level of debt.

It *should* have come as no major surprise that the Greek issue returned with a vengeance in 2015. The euro project has played an instrumental part in destabilising the Greek economy. Firstly, without the euro it simply would not have had access to such vast amounts of cheap money. Secondly, when running into serious trouble the first few times the federalists simply postponed and accentuated the problems and spiral of bad debt by loosening money restrictions even further. Thirdly, the relative strength of the euro over recent years has been hugely at odds with the poorly performing Greek economy. That is synonymous with a structurally disadvantaged Greek export industry. Fourth, Greece has never fulfilled the membership criteria which even the EU integrationists presented as crucial to success when the euro project was marketed. These 'details' continued to be ignored.

And what was the response of the EU integrationists this time? Remorse? Admittance of at least some flaws in the federalist narrative? No. Instead it is communicated that if only Brussels had even more powers and funds, the challenges would be possible to overcome.

The story relating to the migration crisis is much the same. A real problem – the fact that there are a greater number of people willing to migrate from poorer to richer countries than has proven possible to integrate smoothly – has not been met with the unbiased evaluation and necessary compromises it craves but with an unbending unwillingness to concede any point challenging the federalist agenda, up until reactively *compelled* to retreat.

The level of *internal* EU migration first turned politically toxic after the economic downturn partly while prompting fiercer job competition. Things escalated in 2014 when Bulgaria and Romania, after a seven year transition period, were granted the status of full and equal EU members, despite not even having close to the average living standards of other EU countries. Consequently full membership acceptance violated the golden rules broadcasted when the common market was first created. Moreover, despite having lots of catching up to do the Bulgarian and Romanian economies were not even particularly fast growing (unlike for example the Polish and Czech economies). Many Romanians and Bulgarians, entire families, left their homelands in big numbers possibly without the intention of ever coming back. This at a time when schools, hospitals, the housing market and the welfare system were heavily strained in countries that had already welcomed the largest portion of migrants: the UK, Germany and Sweden. The support for the parties of discontent grew but instead of adapting the narrative to realities and concerns on the ground establishment opinion makers typically closed ranks.

Academics that proved willing to dwell on the vague and quite unscientific theories surrounding 'multiculturalism' and 'open door policies' continued to receive huge money grants and plenty of media exposure given an implicit understanding about the conclusions that borders are artificial constructions arrived at through imperialism or chance. Consequently no need to pay heed, ideally all borders should be dissolved and those thinking otherwise are throwback nationalists. This narrative arguably fitted the EU federalist agenda somewhat too well. For years careers could still be built by simply joining the chorus. Some opinion makers – academics, politicians, journalists, think tankers - came almost fresh from universities where the open door mentality had evolved into a mantra. For a while everyone objecting was notoriously - and again a bit too conveniently - labelled a racist.

The *external* migration crisis escalated in 2015 as numerous refugees from the Syrian civil war tried to make their way to start a new life in Europe. Notoriously people drowned when illegally trying to make the crossing from Turkey to Greece. Naturally it was not the first time a war had led to lots of suffering refugees. Previously the typical response had been for every European nation to decide individually how many asylum seekers could be accepted without risking a destabilising political backlash domestically. Efforts beyond that had been focused on making sure life was bearable in the refugee camps bordering the warzone while awaiting a more stable situation in the country at war. This time it was different while the 'open door multiculturalists' were now not only in charge but trapped in their own narrative. For years they had communicated that borders were evil remnants of an obsolete era. Consequently also migration quotas must be considered evil.

Without much warning German Chancellor Angela Merkel declared, in August 2015, it was a humanitarian duty to accept every asylum seeker. She then simply suspended the EU ('Dublin convention') rule that asylum seekers have to seek asylum in the first EU country of arrival. Without leaving any scope for nuance or impact assessment this served as an open invitation for asylum seekers to Germany which pressured other model (internationalist) member states to adopt the same policy. Quite so, soon especially Germany and Sweden accepted unprecedented numbers of migrants. Several countries, including gatekeeping nations such as Greece, were forced to ease their administrative asylum seeker burden, also unprecedented, by simply letting every asylum seeker pass through without vetting; as well as everyone *claiming* to be an asylum seeker from Syria.

Free movement yes

Yet again the EU tried to use political chaos – to no small degree self-inflicted - to assume additional powers. For a while the last remnants of Schengen free movement constraints were effectively removed. The EU federalists also started planning an EU border control supposedly with real clout – and with powers possibly equal to those of member states. The EU also decided to overrule several Eastern European EU member countries unwilling to accept asylum seekers. However, the EU decision could not really be enforced due to an arguably highly predictable political backlash. Some countries, starting with Hungary, simply closed their borders. Even the Swedish government conceded partial defeat and erected border controls between Sweden and Denmark - for the first time since the 1950s.

This political backlash was amplified by amongst others the Paris terrorist attacks in November 2015 and New Year's Eve sexual harassments scandals in both German Cologne and Swedish Kalmar. These scandals were made worse by (failed) information blackout attempts in both countries.

The EU federalist migration interventions have not really satisfied anyone. Numerous struggling migrants have been given hopes that have proven false while unrealistic to fulfil. The prospects of stabilising Syria has deteriorated as many peaceful working age Syrians have moved elsewhere. European natives concerned by safety issues, job market competition as well as an often rapidly changing community demographic have been blatantly disregarded. Moreover, possibly nothing has dented EU voter trust more than the EU opinion maker habit of communicating as if voters cannot handle the truth. Such paternalism underlines a notion, widespread also beforehand, of an 'elite establishment' quite willing to press on even without a clear democratic mandate.

The only ones benefitting from the migration crisis are the European parties of discontent, people smugglers and identity forgers as well as President Putin, who is left more room to manoeuver when Europe is in political disarray.

The story of the EU *is* a story about "ever closer union" in small, often almost unnoticeable steps as when the European Commission snuck through new working rules by switching Treaty articles. Or "big bangs" in EU treaties or in response to a crisis, such as the bailouts or repeal of the Dublin convention relating to asylum seeker rules.

The story of the EU is also, as already mentioned, a tale of diplomatic sophistication – at literally the highest level. By piecemeal expansion, familiarisation, ever expanding (PR) budget and nomination powers as well as the inclusion of key political figures, the EU now touches on most areas of national political life.

There is, however, one problem: voters are now less convinced about the merits of the European Project than at any previous point in its history.

The idealistic zeal of the EU federalists, for quite a while a potent weapon in their hands, has now been stretched to a point when it has started to backfire.

Brussels nevertheless remains talking about birth pangs and how voter discontent can be reduced by even more "EU information". The difference between the 'idealists' and the 'realists' could hardly be greater.

Chapter 2: Dominating vested interests influencing the EU

What you get if you analyse a political system from a purely technical perspective - treaty texts, power relationships between different institutions and formal voting rights - will not only be quite lifeless but pretty much useless if the ambition is a comprehensive understanding.

It is the human operators of the system, the public servants, who really are in command not only of the technicalities just mentioned but also of the general political direction. Consequently a sober, realistic eye to the motives of these operators – especially the vested interests influencing them - is what makes it possible to genuinely understand any bureaucracy. However, for three reasons it is *particularly* important to portray the vested interests – some might prefer to say system biases or hidden agendas - when analysing the EU. Firstly, the EU is one of the most politically powerful organisations on the planet. In a quite direct way its officials already affect the lives of citizens in no less than 28 countries including around 500 million people. Secondly, the distance between the EU institutions and the voters – as well as the closely related transparency problems - is greater than in any other supposedly democratic political system. Thirdly, the system has been designed without setting clear limits to its powers. Instead the Treaty of Rome bidding of "ever closer union" has, by generations of federalists, been interpreted as the very opposite. All this means that the scope for abuse is considerable. In fact, designing a political system with vast political powers, weak links to voters and without stipulating clear power limits is only possible when believing – or feigning to believe – in a romantic notion of human nature. With a realist notion it is synonymous with nothing less than *inviting* abuse. And continuous expansionism as well as immense powers of interpretation. Ironically, the latter will be used not least to combat – or silence – portrayals of the vested interests influencing the system.

Every dominant political group has always exaggerated the influence of others in order to deflect attention from their own influence. This is why the current affairs debate often reeks of a fight against windmills.

For example, today the political right loves to draw weapons against 'socialists' whereas the political left just as eagerly draws weapons against 'Thatcherites'. Few establishment opinion makers seriously challenge the thinking of the centre-ground – despite the fact that *real* power in all major political camps is much closer to the centre-ground than anywhere else.

If really striving to deconstruct contemporary political biases focus must not be on smashing doors that have already been smashed many times before - while pretending they have not. It means smashing the doors that remain closed while politically sensitive *today*. Here goes.

*

2.1 The political centre ground bias

The political right is famously split on the EU, reflecting a clash of interests. This partly reflects that the business community, the main financier of right-wing party election campaigns, is in itself split. To simplify, one group, dominated by multinational firms, sees the EU as an entity facilitating trade in new places while there are no product and service duties within the EU, and while one point of entry in many ways serves as a legal passport (even if not all) to operations also in other member states. The other group, which includes many small and medium-sized enterprises, is more sceptical; they may only engage in limited export activities but are nevertheless faced with a double set of rules (national and supranational). This adds costs. Among industries that for political reasons have been regulated more than others, for example selected parts of the finance industry, scepticism has sometimes increased despite the benefit these sectors enjoy from more access to the European market.

Some even argue that the ever-increasing stock of EU regulations and directives is so burdensome and restricted that the EU of the 21st century has negated many of the EU of the 1990s helped to create. For this business group, labour market policies, environment policies and health and safety policies are frequently seen as an alibi for a covert left-wing, 'anti-business' agenda.

Within the most *thriving* parts of the business community the attitude to economic migration has for a long time been generally positive - it keep wages down, and enlarges the pool of potential workers. If, on the other hand, immigration is considered to put additional pressure on the welfare system (and increase the tax burden), the attitude can be more ambivalent. Small business owners further down the value chain are typically more hesitant, especially if immigrants set up competing businesses themselves.

Also, corporations which possess lots of spare money that can be used for lobbying purposes, and to impose regulations unfavourable to small and medium sized competitors, tend to exert much more influence over EU legislation than over legislation passed in national parliaments (partly due the greater anonymity, more about this later). The reverse is true for corporations without such money. Indeed, even legislation that affects large and small businesses alike is more burdensome to the smaller organisations as adherence to new rules will take more relative focus from other business activities.

The dividing lines within the business community – the most important one are often poorly reflected in the official communications of the major employers' organisations. The reason is that these groups are usually dominated by the global – and therefore typically more EU-friendly - companies.

The attitude towards the EU has always been divided also on the political left, mainly reflecting splits within the trades unions, the main Labour party funders. Trades unions associated with flourishing export-oriented industries have often welcomed an expanded internal market. Boosted sales and company growth substantially improves the negotiating position when discussing salaries and other working conditions. Company growth might also mean additional job opportunities and additional trades union members. For the reverse reasons trades unions associated with less competitive industries have tended to be more protectionist and Eurosceptic (these have usually also provided the power base for the Labour 'radicals', those that, contrary to the Labour moderates, dispute that free trade benefits the working class). Economic migration has also been a massive internal challenge for unions. On the one hand, the commitment to international solidarity with workers everywhere, on the other the fear of wages being undercut and jobs lost to foreigners. This tension has been particularly hard to manage for unions during periods of economic downturn, when competition on the labour market has been particularly fierce.

Naturally, the level of labour market legislation has also influenced trade unions' attitudes towards the EU. Most trades unions are favourably disposed towards stricter labour market legislation but not always at the EU level. Some trades unions might feel that they exert greater individual influence at the national level, especially so if the 'capitalist' pressure groups are easier to neutralise.

Since anonymity, as touched upon before, favours the cash rich pressure groups there can also be an element of policy collusion between the well capitalised trade unions and the well capitalised employer organisations. If these can agree on a set of legislation that protects the status quo both sides might benefit at the cost of the smaller market participants trying to break through.

Stating the obvious, EU scepticism on the left has grown when it has perceived that the right has expanded its influence within the EU – and vice versa. A clear trend is that the political left, over time, has turned more positive towards the EU as it has moved from being not much more than a promoter of free trade into an entity with a broad (interventionist) political mandate. The consequence of the latter is that the EU's original prime focus area, economic collaboration, has developed into merely one of many programme areas. The reverse logic, again, applies to the political right. This dynamic, however, has now been complicated by the eurozone crisis, which has triggered a wave of EU-mandated 'austerity' measures.

Only among the centre parties has the view of the EU *not* been divided at all, but rather remained wholly enthusiastic. The first of two major reasons (the second reason is covered under the next headline 'Internationalist peace paradigm bias') is that international member organisations such as the EU (and the UN) almost by definition are driven by compromise and thereby a centrist agenda. This is directly illustrated when most decisions are taken. It is also illustrated in top job appointments. Candidates perceived as either too right-wing or too left-wing are simply blocked. Only candidates that are not anathema on either political side can muddle through a selection process. This helps to explain why no President of the Commission has belonged to anything other than the progressive centre-left or centre-right. Sometimes a less important post can be conceded to the left but only if a post with a similar standing is simultaneously conceded to the right. Even so the balance of power remains firmly within the political centre.

The second major reason is that the 'internationalist' agenda, which took shape in the second half of the 19th century, is a creation which already from the start was tailor-made to advance the centrist agenda. Certainly, it was the more right-wing classical liberals that initiated the process[17]. This was done by orchestrating the removal of the trade barriers that had been deeply coupled with international trade during the royal era. In 1860 the Cobden-Chevalier agreement – a landmark trade deal -was signed by the UK and France. A number of customs duties were dramatically reduced. In addition, a so called most-favoured-nation-paragraph dictated that if one party concluded a tariff reduction agreement with a third country, the other party would also be covered. In that spirit, free trade agreements were signed between most European states during the decades that followed. As a consequence, by the turn of the century the greater part of (Western) Europe had developed into something quite close to a free trade zone. Now as then agricultural tariffs were the main exception to the rule. These had been lowered but were raised when the transport revolution made it possible for US farming products to sell competitively on the European markets.

However, not long afterwards, the Liberal party began its transformation from classic liberalism to social liberalism. This in direct response to the growth of trades union and the interlinked and gradual democratic breakthrough[18]. A new ideological pretext was needed that on the one hand defended international economic cooperation and on the other hand promoted a rapidly changing and expanding social agenda.

It was in this political context that free trade was linked to the idea of how to achieve peace. Through more international trade, countries would be tied more closely together not merely to promote economic growth but also to prevent war. Economic cooperation, in other words, was in *everyone's* interest - not merely in the interest of the industrialists and the business community (Cobden had argued this all along).

Added to this was the strong zeitgeist belief that difficult political problems could be resolved through scientific analysis and rational debate. Social problems should no longer be dealt with by talking about decaying morals but instead by consulting *academic* studies of deprivation and ill-health. According to the new way of thinking also international tension could be reduced by a scientific approach. Previous generations had been sabre rattling to deter potential enemies but many now started arguing this had *created* hostility. If government leaders of other countries do not feel threatened they will not attack. The suggested way to go is therefore disarmament.

This line of thinking was also strongly linked to the increasingly popular idea that the environment rather than hereditary traits decide individual human qualities - including the level of human aggressiveness[19]. If the personality is shaped by the environment rather than established at birth it is of crucial importance to make sure that the environment supports and nurtures the good qualities of every individual, including other Heads of Government. In the modern scientific era these Heads of Government would be educated, rational and fully aware that war tends to lead to destruction and deprivation rather than peace and welfare. Through appeasement they would cease to be even potential enemies.

Voilá, an *internationalist progressive* pattern of thought had been established[20]. Like all political ideologies, this one too laid claim to promoting both peace and prosperity. The novelty was the notable centrist nature of the new, internationalist movement - in terms of both reasoning and final political verdicts. The latter was illustrated by close to all lines of reasoning ending up in middle-of-the-road conclusions, for example the denunciation of both the 'militarist right' and the 'revolutionary left'.

A key to understanding the EU is to understand that its ideological roots, the federalist logic underpinning it, is clearly centrist/progressive. The drivers behind the European project have also, with remarkably few exceptions, been found among people advocating a centrist – progressive - political agenda.

A key to understanding the present *debate* surrounding the EU is to realise that it is neither dominated by the right nor (as it is still often said) the left. Rather it is, as never before, dominated by the political centre. As all major political parties are now fighting for the centre ground it is the ideological twists and turns that support the centre that prevails over the ideological twist and turns supporting all other ideological camps. This explains why substantial opposition to the ideology underpinning the EU is not presented by the major parties. In fact, the absence of a vigorous debate within the so called establishment is a direct reflection of the fact that the political centre is stronger today than in any previous era in the history of politics.

Sure, sometimes the centre of gravity tips to the right, like when the ECJ ruled against unions in successive cases in the mid-noughties (Laval, Viking, Ruffert) or when the Commission instructs France to cut its spending. Sometimes to the left, like in the case of the Working Time Directive or the Financial Transaction Tax. However, the main direction of the EU has for quite some time been unmistakeably centrist.

Also, the centrist social liberal view on 'controlling the market', which permeates so much of the current EU thinking, fits hand in glove with the modern internationalist agenda[21]. Unlike the far left, control is executed through a watching state eye rather than through full nationalisation. In practice this means a lot of regulatory centralisation, including a steady stream of new laws and agencies, while still leaving political cover for the "free market." In Germany, this is known as the "social market economy" – though even there, the term means different things in different political camps, showing what a politically useful balancing act this is.

*

2.2 Career bias

Looking into the armies of EU dependants – there are four – goes a long way in mapping the EU support system. The army of direct dependants includes people straightforwardly employed in any of the expansive EU web of institutions, agencies, regulatory bodies, executive bodies, special EU committees and other quangos.

The EU people are well looked after through generous salaries, expat allowances, household allowances, travel expenses, pension agreements, free school fees for children, golden parachutes as well as highly generous tax benefits (around 16 percent on average). In most EU countries, the compensation package is more generous than it is for national politicians.[22][23]

Also for reasons other than financial, an international life is attractive to many people. With approximately 50,000 direct employees and a rotation of posts typical of international organisations, the EU complex today comprises a whole employment industry.

This army also includes EU grant recipients on the national level such as farmers, social cohesion fund recipients, universities, think tanks, media outlets as well as all sorts of associations within the cultural sphere.

A second army of indirect dependants includes tens of thousands of member state public servants; administrators and coordinators whose jobs will be lost if the EU breaks apart.

For politicians and civil servants in all camps the EU has also, over the last decade, developed into a central gateway to career, remuneration, pension and consultation. It does not help that there might be a 'top table syndrome' among diplomats, an expression used by economist Roger Bootle, meaning that the urge to be invited to the circle of the most internationally important cloud the judgement.[24]

Which official is going to oppose the EU if a top international job is in the offing – meaning higher salary, lower tax and greater prestige? Is it reasonable to expect that officials in national ministries or authorities – whose employment is based on the existence of the EU – can have anything other than a positive attitude to the EU?

The army of indirect dependents also includes professors, lawyers, EU correspondents and many others who, even if not subsidised by EU money, build careers through EU specialisation.

A third army of dependants includes lobbyists: corporate lobbyists, trade union lobbyists and NGO lobbyists. These are often well-funded professionals who are well aware that it is much easier to influence the legislation machinery at the supranational level than at the national level. Why? Simply because dealings are more anonymous and less scrutinized. Crucially, large corporations can also collide to create legislation and a regulatory framework that benefits large players over small.

The fourth army is an auxiliary army which includes top brass member state public servants. This army has grown steadily as the EU has developed into a central career and remuneration gateway. Which official is going to oppose the EU if a top international job is in the offing – perhaps meaning higher salary, lower tax, more prestige and (again) less scrutiny? This is the most politically important army as it includes precisely those politicians and civil servants who were supposed to provide member state counterweight to EU demands.

Given these vested interests, is it really surprising that responses from member state public servants are often comically weak when new EU centralisation initiatives are presented? Is it strange that most EU legislation proposals, EU project evaluations and EU books end with expressions of general support when most "EU experts" are themselves part of the EU umbrella? Is it strange that Brussels, similar to Washington, has turned into a lobbyist Mecca?

*

2.3 Great power bias

The reason Germany, the UK and France exercise exceptional influence within the EU is, self-evidently, due to a greater population and therefore greater voting power within most EU-institutions. But it is not only a question of population size. Together the economies of these three countries are, in terms of GDP, larger than the economies of all the remaining 25 EU countries put together. The latter is the main reason important *national* decisions in Berlin, Paris and London can influence all other member states. That is also why corresponding decisions in Copenhagen, Lisbon and Bucharest might not make the headlines even in neighbouring countries. It is because of this gap in power basics that alliances between small and medium-sized countries do not tend to suffice to neutralise the corresponding strength of the three great powers. Instead, each small country tends to trail the single great power which is best thought to represent its own interests. That boosts the great powers even further. The end result of all this is that the interaction between Germany, the UK and France usually determines in which way the EU develops.

After the fall of the Soviet Union and the almost simultaneous fall of Margaret Thatcher, pronounced centre-right or centre-left governments have succeeded each other in Germany, France as well as in the UK. For almost two decades all governments in all three countries also eagerly embraced the Brussels agenda. It is telling that it is precisely during this period - when the three countries have been in more political accord than perhaps ever before - that the EU powers have expanded *massively*. It is necessary to arrive almost to the present day, and the David Cameron government elected in 2010, to find some major EU policy discrepancy between the great power governments. It is also telling that not even the David Cameron government of 2010-2015, an alliance between the Conservatives and the Liberal Democrats, was *voted in* with an EU platform that deviated much from the EU platform of predecessors

Gordon Brown and Tony Blair. The change took place reactively and gradually *after* being voted in. Spectacularly, this happened as a result of the growing popular EU discontent and the closely linked Ukip advances. The simultaneous weakening of the Liberal Democrats, a party which has so far consistently stuck to its EU guns, has also been important.

*

2.4 Macroeconomic bias and the unholy alliance between politicians and banks

Many have already suggested that the EU federalists have created the Euro for political rather than economic reasons. There are strong reasons, accounted for below, to support this claim. Then again, a high degree of intervention on the monetary market is by no means exclusive for the EU federalists. Far reaching monetary intervention has for decades been a hallmark of the policies also of individual EU member states. However, the EU federalists have taken these policies, arguably excessive already among many member states, to a yet higher level.

A quick glance at the historic shifts in macroeconomic policy helps to put the monetary policies, including the euro project, into perspective. States borrowing lots of money is far from a novelty. States-borrowing-to-fight-wars has notoriously been done many times in history. Behind that policy there were no long-winded explanations besides emotional talk about the honour of the nation. Pay up and fight or die. The era of the great depression saw the introduction of another type of macroeconomic policy: borrow-and-invest-in-infrastructure-so-that-the-unemployed-get-temporary-jobs-and-do-not-starve. It is not quite right to attach that change of policy only to common sense. True, people could not be allowed to starve and not only for ethical reasons. Also the risk of riots had to be taken into consideration. However, the economy had been in dire straits many times before – and people poor - without leaders having resorted to fiscal intervention. Until the democratic breakthrough such problems had typically been tackled by making the terms of the poor law somewhat more liberal (temporarily). What was new was the political strengthening of the working class. With industrialisation and the democratic breakthrough the trade unions exercised substantial political clout. When the state administrators decided to fund large (infrastructure) projects the trade union members were most often the main beneficiaries. The new era of fiscal activism was directly related to this circumstance.

The last decades, starting with the 1980s, have yet again seen the adoption of a novel macroeconomic policy: borrow-and-lend-so-banks-and-voters-can-borrow-and-spend. This policy means that the governments, instead of making investment decisions themselves, are using the central banks to offer commercial banks artificially low interest in order for them and their borrowers to make investment and consumptions decisions. Ideally, the industrial wheels of society will then keep spinning.

The reason fiscal activism is typically supported by the political left and monetary activism by the political right has, as always, primarily to do with who benefits. Fiscal activism benefits not only trade unions but also state officials. To realise fiscal activism in practice the number of state administrators – planners including academics – has to be expanded. Monetary activism empowers, at least temporarily, both the big end-consumer lenders and numerous borrowers: banks, building societies and mortgage holders. Temporarily both types of activism can benefit incumbent governments as demand is (artificially) boosted which pushes up growth figures.

It is the socio-economic shift, the political strengthening of the house-owning middle class, which explains why monetary intervention now tends to be more in vogue than fiscal intervention. Much has already been written about the industrial automation having reduced the relative demand for blue-collar workers at the same time as the relative importance of traditional conveyor belt industries has lost ground to more knowledge-intensive industries. More people have had to be educated and more people have also moved up the income brackets. This is why the working class is now outnumbered by the typically home owning middle class. As a direct consequence governments reach (buy) a wider group of voters if tampering with housing policies than by commissioning the building projects that leads to more jobs for trade union members.

The logic outlined ultimately explains why housing policies, including central bank policies and mortgage lending practices, have changed so spectacularly since the 1980s. To a degree previously unheard of states have intervened through artificially low interest (mortgage) rates and much looser mortgage repayment conditions. In addition, far-reaching government guarantees have been extended to banks and building societies meaning that if mortgage holders do not manage to honour their debts the state (taxpayer) will foot the bill. After removing the default risk from banks and building societies lending has, naturally, exploded.

Groups get special treatment if well organised (banks) or extra important come election day (mortgage holders). Groups without a collective voice, taxpayers and savers, are made to assume - largely unknowingly - the default risk.

The *officially* declared purpose of the monetary policies has been to help more people onto the housing ladder.

The support for this 'modern' line of monetary policy has now for a long time been so strong and widespread that it, in practice, has been more or less impossible for politicians to deviate and still hope to be elected. The guilt for hugely inflaming the bubble, therefore, has to be shared between politicians of all flavours, the central bank, commercial banks, as well as academics supporting the 'generous' housing policies. The political and commercial forces defending the narrative have been so strong that the house price bubble has really been unavoidable (this in turn reflect the short term horizons of both politicians and CEOs).

A mitigating circumstance for the 'guilty' parties is that the forces of mass psychology should not be underestimated. The perhaps vast majority who have jumped on the bandwagon have done so simply while convinced that everyone else cannot be wrong (still the case). A mitigating circumstance for mortgage holders, even if crucial stakeholders, were that they were arguably duped (many still are) to think that the policies that for years had helped politicians (to be elected) and banks (to profit massively) were sustainable. However, mitigating circumstances or not, the effects have been none the less harmful.

The absence of an honest debate afterwards, practically impossible when all pillars of society are in on it, has also hindered a healthy readjustment. In fact, healthy readjustment has been proactively thwarted. While admitting no major flaw in the earlier monetary and housing policies the medicine prescribed has been to reach even deeper into the state coffers (again meaning the coffers of taxpayers and savers) in order to keep stoking the fire and *avoid* in the end unavoidable adjustments.

Enter the euro project.

Before Euro cooperation, countries such as Greece, Portugal, Spain, Italy, Cyprus and Ireland had, of course, their own currencies. Their credit rating on the money market was worse than that of, for example Germany, the UK or Sweden. The reason was that their national finances were less sound. The latter was reflected by lenders on the international loan market requiring higher loan interest. The states borrowed, but were forced to take into account not only that it was expensive but also that there was no one else to blame if questionable borrowing ended in national bankruptcy. At times international lenders sounded a borrowing retreat, well aware that they would lose out if national bankruptcy really turned into a fact. Naturally, even then it was possible to borrow 'too much', for example by manoeuvring and fiddling with the national accounts. Yet, an upper limit on borrowing and debt did exist.

Through Euro cooperation, the European Central Bank (backed up by mighty Germany) accepted a position as guarantor of the eurozone states, including the high-risk countries. Countries that had systematically offended against the previously sanctified convergence criteria of the Maastricht Treaty, including the 'essential' criterion that national debt must not exceed 60 percent of GNP, were not merely accepted but *encouraged* to enter the eurozone.

As the high-risk countries offered higher interest rates, but were suddenly backed by the European Central Bank, international lenders were given strong financial incentives to lend money to these very countries. Not without reason the market soon ceased to regard these countries as high-risk countries. As a direct result, interest rates in Greece, Portugal, Spain, Italy, Cyprus and Ireland fell. Despite no structural changes in these economies the governments could borrow considerably more money than before, and at a lower price.

Subsequently, Greece, Portugal, Spain, Italy, Cyprus and Ireland could borrow money just as cheaply as Germany (almost free). This was an opportunity that was also used with gusto. Precisely as in northern Europe (and the USA), a large proportion of the money borrowed was used to buy even more electoral support through even more monetary intervention. As house prices rose, Greeks, Irish, Cypriots and Portuguese felt richer for every year that passed. Many bought German cars and French wine. Everything completely in line with the intentions of the Euro architects. 'The system is stimulating itself. This is what happens when markets are merged. Everybody is happy and pleased!'

Of course, both the national debt and property prices rose rapidly, but if anyone raised doubts the ECB repeated its guarantee promises: 'The risk is minimal, the balance sheet of the ECB - which is guaranteed by Germany - will take all the knocks'. For people caught up in this line of reasoning it seemed beneficial to 'forget' the rules that were put so much weight upon when the euro project was constructed. 'Yes, we have now infringed the convergence criteria, but everything is going like clockwork. Why not use a winning formula?'

At this point the European Central Bank had in effect turned into a 'holding company' which started to draw on its core resources to uphold troubled subsidiaries. However, just as previously in the history of economics, bounteous lending works until the lenders get cold feet and start questioning the solidity of the whole structure. The sums at stake grew to a point when the entire system began to come into question – and the banks began to question the guarantee commitments. It got really bumpy at the start of the recession when the growth forecasts were dramatically cut. Thereafter it was evident that many eurozone members would not be able to service their debts themselves. The European bubble burst when German taxpayers (electors) also began to grumble big-time. At this point the tune changed. The European Central Bank, in co-operation with the International Monetary Fund, *now* started demanding 'necessary' structural reforms in order to extend further loans.

It takes a great amount of wishful political thinking to dispute that structural reforms really were and are necessary. However, structural reforms, with the purpose of balancing the budget, had been necessary for years beforehand including when the Greeks were signed up to the euro project. It had then suited the EU expansionists to turn a blind eye.

The Greeks criticised the EU – and in particular Germany – for having pulled them into a euro project which had proved financially disastrous. It was certainly true that the power people in Brussels almost unanimously had worked strenuously to pull in as many countries in the euro project as possible – more or less regardless of economic conditions. However, blaming the Germans was only partially true. The German political class with strong ties to EU and Brussels had certainly backed the euro project. Also, many within the German export industry had offered strong backing. The reason is that countries such as Greece and Italy could, as long as they had independent currencies, partly offset high German productivity by currency devaluation. These countries gained a cost advantage which vanished with the euro. This means that the euro boosted the competitiveness of German exporters within the eurozone.

On the other hand, after the German pre-war (printing press and inflation) experience no German government has been inclined to risk the potential negative effects of excessive lending. The reason is that German taxpayers, the ultimate guarantors of government debt, have reacted negatively already when homespun debt levels have grown. In addition, savers of money have been strongly opposed to loose monetary policy as this has resulted in dwindling interest rate returns and possibly inflationary pressure in the long run. The eurozone project has been a let down on both these accounts. It has turned German taxpayers into the ultimate guarantors of everybody's debt, whereas the loose monetary policies of the European Central Bank have made nonsense of the yield expectations of money savers. Not surprisingly, and yet again certainly not without merit, many German electors have subsequently showed great irritation at having to bail out 'over-paid and over-consuming Greeks'.

This means that Germans have been split over the eurozone project, even so within the ranks of the politically crucial middle class. However, German political and industrial factions of Germany, those that supported the euro, would not have got its way without France. Next to the EU institutions themselves France had all along been the main driver and architect of the eurozone project. Also many politicians (and academics) within the southern European countries were strong backers of the euro project right until the downturn. The euro project, a source for easy money and an at least temporary redistributor of wealth from northern to southern Europe, was simply too hard to resist. However, the southern countries have been and still are peripheral to what is decided in Brussels. Without French and partial German backing they would never have had a chance to create the eurozone.

It is probably right to conclude that blame in the Greek soap opera needs to be shared. The EU institutions and the Northern European interest groups driving the EU expansionist agenda have arguably behaved like parents spoiling their children rotten as long as they are cute and love you for it; while still expecting impeccable manners and frugality when the children turn into teenagers and things easily get out of hand. Many Greek politicians have too readily *assumed* the very role of children seeking immediate gratification without thinking about tomorrow. This approach was arguably brought to an extreme point in July 2015 when Greek Prime Minister Alexis Tsipras and Finance Minister Yanis Varoufakis, in effect, asked voters (in a referendum) if they wanted to repay the creditors of Greece what the country of Greece had borrowed and promised to repay. There is no small irony in this turn of events. Not only was the eurozone expanded for the wrong reasons; it was then put under strain for the wrong reasons.

Spearheaded by the President of the EU Commission, Jean-Claude Juncker, the integrationists repeatedly linked euro membership both to economic growth and EU membership: "If they vote No, it would be disastrous for the future.. No would mean ... they are saying No to Europe."[25]

The Greek people did say no, όχι, but possibly mainly while wanting to bloody the nose of the EU federalists and Greek establishment politicians.

In the end the challengers still recanted and almost unconditionally accepted the terms set in Brussels, thereby exposing that the referendum was primarily an attempt to strengthen the bargaining position. That attempt failed miserably. Seemingly also the challengers believed the EU federalist narrative that it would be an even worse disaster to leave the eurozone than to stay within.

What followed could now be considered a classic EU tale. As a response to the crisis a substantial amount of Greek sovereignty was transferred to Brussels (a significant portion of Greek assets were handed over for administration by the EU institutions). Then yet another bailout programme was launched which was funded by the EU taxpayers.

So, is there any merit in the federalist scaremongering that this was an 'absolutely necessary' outcome and that leaving the eurozone would make a bad situation even worse? The integrationists downplay or simply ignore many strong counterarguments. Firstly, as a general strategy it is highly questionable to remedy a problem that to a large degree was created by too much control from the top by even more control from the top. Secondly, throwing good money after bad - to a country that is famous for its tax evasion, shadow economy and for being a serial defaulter – might not be the best use of taxpayer money. Thirdly, the problem that already caused so much strain, the problem of having a euro member that actually does not fulfil the membership criteria, remains unsolved. Fourth, if separating its weakest member, Greece, from the euro project there would immediately be much less uncertainty about the demand for future bailout money. The rest of the eurozone would then instantaneously be standing on a much healthier financial footing. Yes, it would send the signal to other members that if also they violated the membership criteria they risked being kicked out. That would indeed be the right signal to send, what is otherwise the point of having such criteria? Fifth, reintroducing the drachma would, de facto, mean an immediate and substantial currency devaluation. That would give the Greek export and tourist industry a much needed boost. Sixth, it would still be perfectly possible for Greece to rejoin the eurozone at a future point, when and if the country met the membership criteria. Seventh, leaving the Eurozone would not mean leaving the European Union. Why would it? The argument that the preservation of the euro project is vital to also preserving the European Union was certainly not used when the EU was created in the 1990s, even though the euro project was then already much discussed. Moreover, many other EU members outside the eurozone are famously doing better, economically, than those within.

A Greek exit from the eurozone would potentially offer both Greece and the euro project a fresh start, especially if coupled with debt write downs. The latter would mean a lot to Greece and might also benefit the creditors (EU taxpayers). How so? A large portion of the debts are highly unlikely to be repaid anyway and the risk of future bailouts would vanish.

Another counterargument to the remedy chosen is that yet again the structural solutions to the real issues have been simply put off. There can be little doubt there will be yet another Greek episode.

Certainly, after having accumulated a disastrous level of debt there is no easy, immediate way going forward but the EU integrationists' refusal to seriously consider the counterarguments manifests, yet again, that the integrationist agenda is *the* top priority. Even when people's livelihoods and futures are at stake.

So, has the development, at any point, encouraged reflection and a degree of remorse in Brussels? Not at all. The leading figures of the EU have never admitted *any* prime responsibility – except possibly a failure in not having advanced the integrationist agenda at greater speed. Before the election to the European Parliament in May 2014, José Barroso (President of the EU Commission 2004–2014) travelled around Europe holding lectures in which he asserted that the crisis, up until that point, was the result of an irresponsible financial sector and that national governments had incurred too much debt. In such a lecture in London[26], he conveniently claimed that part of the problem was that the EU had *not* exercised any macroeconomic influence at all during the crisis years. He then, again, 'forgot' to mention that the record levels of debt incurred by the high-risk countries would have been impossible if the European Central Bank had not guaranteed all the Euro-dominated government bonds. No word either about the EU institutions having contributed to subsidising the 'too-big-to-fail' banking sector at the expense of the taxpayers.

According to Mr Barroso – and his many sympathisers, including Jean-Claude Juncker – the recklessness that caused the Euro crisis was only to be found among banks. For the EU federalists, there are three main reasons to make the banking sector assume all the blame. The most obvious one is that no finger will point in their own direction if they successfully nominate a scapegoat. Despite its major role in creating the mess the EU leaders have maintained that the EU, through its many subsequent support programmes, have saved particularly troubled countries like Ireland, Greece and Cyprus. The second reason is that the euro project rests heavily on that belief being upheld. If it is not, if it is generally understood that the EU federalists have themselves played a major role in aggravating the crisis, then the entire project risks crumbling. The third reason, closely related to the second, is that from a Brussels political power perspective the Euro has indeed been a remarkably useful instrument in realising the ambition to transfer macroeconomic influence from national governments to itself.

"The EU made significant progress [in 2014] towards a banking union, restoring confidence, ending the era of taxpayers having to pay for the mistakes of banks and enabling the financial sector to start lending again." (Jean-Claude Juncker not long before the escalation of the Greek crisis).[27]

Given that the EU federalist narrative has been widely believed for years, the crisis response has been close to inevitable. By maintaining that the recession was so long and deep as a result of the fact that the EU did not exercise sufficient influence over fiscal policy, it follows naturally to argue that a *yet further* deepening is necessary. It follows almost as naturally to argue the need to broaden the EU's supervisory mandate over the banking sector – although *without* it afflicting the lending capabilities of the banking sector.

It is precisely in this way that EU federalists such as Mr Barroso and Mr Juncker have both argued and acted. During Barroso's period in office, an area of carpet-bombing has been presented involving amongst others the following macroeconomic initiatives; The Stability and Growth Pact. The Fiscal Pact. The Bank Union. The European Term. Six-pack. Two-pack. Europlus-pact. Long-term refinancing operation (LTRO). European Financial Stability Facility. Outright monetary transactions (OMT). Asset-backed securities (ABS) purchase programme. Quantitative Easing (QE) the modern (virtual money) equivalent of money printing. The common theme in all these initiatives is to extend financial overview or further credit or further guarantees to governments in debt.

Elegant terminology is used to hide the intentions behind these programmes which in practice have fundamentally changed the ECB rules. Capital requirements for Central Banks have been slackened to allow *yet further lending*. The ABS programme means that the European Central Bank is now allowed to accept securities as collateral that previously were disallowed while considered by many as 'trash assets'. Such changes violate the ECB mandate as stipulated in the Maastricht Treaty. In practice this has proven unimportant. The EU federalists – including the ECB management - are their own judges. Moreover, in the name of 'solidarity' several of the just mentioned 'rescue packages' have been backed up also by countries outside the eurozone. This means that the resources in the least damaged economies are now also drawn upon to keep the system going.

The continued massive support for ECB lending in combination with the previously mentioned difficulties of getting out of a debt spiral has created a situation when only one eurozone country has, at least for a considerable period of time, managed to follow the 60 percent rule (Finland – and just barely). During the 1990s this rule was used to sell Euro cooperation among those people who were sceptical about the sustainability of the European project (quite a few did indeed foresee the troubles to come but they were conveniently ignored). It was then firmly promised that the rule would never be broken.

The result after all these years of 'generous' lending? Money has been used as a band aid, making it possible to further postpone the structural reforms and price corrections painfully necessary after the 'golden days' of borrowing and consumption hysteria. At the same time even more debt has been accumulated. The lion's share of the serious default risk has been transferred from private banks (which otherwise had pulled out long ago) to (guarantor) EU institutions and thereby, ultimately, to taxpayers.

Besides widening the scope of the ECB the EU federalists have reacted to the economic downturn by also broadening the EU supervisory mandate over the banks (at the cost of national supervisors). Moreover, the EU leaders have diligently shifted the responsibility for control from one authority to another (numerous supervisory authorities existed also before the recession). The practical consequences are often unclear. Sometimes changes might have been made solely to extend the political mandate. There are also reasons to suspect that mandates sometimes are moved around in order to signal executive determination. Some member states may press for changes in order to raise rivals costs[28] or to cater regulations to the needs of interest groups whose support might be useful during an election.[29] Against opposing interest groups regulators might also devise new proposals as a bargaining tool; to make it look as if they gain ground when the proposals are subsequently watered down.

One tangible consequence of the new rules is that the regulations that safeguard the financial system have been tightened up. In practice, this has primarily manifested itself in stricter capital adequacy and accounting requirements. In this case the EU federalists take advantage of the fact that the average voter has difficulty in distinguishing one type of banking activity from another. Such regulations are usually *not* aimed at reducing risk connected with loan operations; the part of the financial services sector that has played the leading role during this business cycle. Instead, the capital requirements connected with lending have instead been slackened yet further in order to encourage lending activities. The tightening regulations that the EU spokespersons want to talk about as crisis-will-not-happen-again-remedies are to a high degree aimed at risk connected with the *securities business* – despite the only indirect involvement of the securities business during the crisis (as money was made artificially cheap and the interest on holding money close to zero, considerable sums were redirected to the stock market; which was thereby also artificially boosted).

It not difficult to conclude that the EU's crisis management policies almost completely fail to touch the core problem. Whereas the borrowing and consumption frenzy – and the reasoning underpinning it - has now been criticised outside the EU sphere, it remains holy ground within. Many federalists still have the stomach to claim that the euro project has had a *stabilising* effect; and that things would have been even worse without it.

From the federalist power perspective these types of remarks are actually, despite arguably grotesque, highly rational. The impact of the real facts has so far proved to be small. The crude but convenient EU federalist narrative, that the financial sector is the sole villain while the political sphere has acted as a helpful repairman, is still marketable. How is this possible? Because it is backed up by the army of powerful people in authority who have invested prestige in the EU and thereby also in the euro project.

At long last many voters, also within the Eurozone, have started suspecting that something is amiss. Then again, the area is complex and the political smokescreens come thick and fast. By spreading uncertainty the EU locomotive can, as usual, force its way forward.

It is certainly true that there has never been any *ideological* love between the EU federalists and the banking sector. That alliance has been – and is – an unholy one. The EU federalists (as well as many EU member state politicians) have needed the banks to implement their 'generous' vote-catching loan policies. Building societies and banks have for several decades made heaps of money out of this need.

It is still because of political intervention that the markets have been distorted to a degree that banks that have maintained more rigid banking standards, during the era of easy money, have lost market shares. This has created a situation when such banks, in a sense, have not fulfilled their duty to their shareholders (of maximising profits). Combine this incentive structure with the typically short-term planning horizon of the finance industry – which for unrelated reasons often does not stretch further than to the next quarterly report – and it is scarcely surprising that almost all the banks have acted as the state's oh so willing fellow travellers.

The understanding between the banks and the politicians has been and still is a tacit one. The banks remain silent when the EU federalists claim they are innocent of any guilt whatsoever and instead blame the crisis entirely on the banks. Banks are also silent when the EU federalists have the audacity to add that the interventionists are rescuers. In exchange for the silence the banks can continue to reap the financial profits of the, despite everything, remarkably intact monetary policies.

The perhaps greatest irony of all is that the massive level of *political* EU intervention, despite being intended to *alleviate* the recession, has prevented market adaptation of interest rates, exchange rates, house prices as well as share prices. This has left the economy hanging. It is actually not the least surprising that especially the eurozone has been in a permanent state of limbo for years. There is every reason to believe that the new macroeconomic paradigm, without which the euro project had been impossible, has deepened and prolonged rather than eased the recession.

It is worth noting how macroeconomics in today's social liberal society differs from both the classic societies of the left and the right. In the left-wing society, the market is so strictly regulated that it fixes a sharp boundary for both speculation and lending. In the classic right-wing society, speculation and lending are allowed but if it goes wrong excessive speculators and borrowers need to assume the responsibility themselves. This means that periods of borrowing- and consumption hysteria are followed by adjustments including price revision and 'creative destruction'.

The EU leaders have chosen a hybrid line. Nothing else can be expected in a middle-class society; on the other hand, the *choice of* hybrid line is noteworthy. In close collaboration with a number of national governments, the EU federalists have chosen to allow governments – and indirectly mortgage holders – to borrow wildly without themselves having to face the consequences of excessive borrowing and consumption. Arguably the fiscal hybrid line chosen combines some of the worst aspects of the regulated market with some of the worst aspects of the free market

This makes it indeed questionable to talk about the EU as an economic association in which excellence and specialisation is rewarded. Possibly it is more correct to talk about the EU as a political centralisation project which uses the *memory* of a previously useful economic association as an alibi for further political centralisation.

*

2.5 Idealist peace paradigm bias and the unholy EU alliance between right and left

It is indeed easy to argue that there was something genuinely sound, excepting agricultural policy, about the initial European project. The aim of the enterprise – free trade of goods and services and free movement of capital and labour – served a clear, limited and easily understandable purpose. The most accomplished industries in each country, the key industries, would flourish and thereby stand completely on their own feet. This would benefit both employers and employees – and society at large - thereby making it possible to avoid the traditional left-right divide. The principal political struggle would instead play out between, on the one side, employers and employees in vital competitive industries and, on the other, employers and employees in industries that found it difficult to hold their own on an open market. However, the choice of having this division instead was a responsible one as there can be little doubt that it boosts long term growth- and employment levels; while simultaneously building in incentives for reinvention of organisations that had grown stale and complacent.

There was certainly a strong peace aspect connected to the European project also between the 1950s and early 1990s but of a totally different nature from today. During the decades after WW2, when people still remembered how the negative economic development of the 1930s had paved the way for parties of discontent, there was a clear understanding that economic growth is vital to economic stability. There was an equally

59

clear understanding that economic growth is also what ultimately makes it possible to maintain a deterrent military capacity. Consequently the EC was considered to promote peace simply by focusing wholeheartedly on promoting economic cooperation. No realist - which regardless of political camp included most dominant politicians across Europe - doubted that it was a totally different organisation, Nato, that ultimately dissuaded any short term potential aggressors. Fresh in people's memories was moreover how the internationalist mindset had failed miserably in preventing WWII.

Certainly, internationalist had its politically strong advocators also between the 1950s and early 1990s but as long as the Soviet threat seemed imminent they could not outweigh the typically realist heads of Government. Even if the 'soft' approach to peace could sound seductive few western world leaders *really* thought that it could hold the Russians at bay. Even the leaders in a supposedly neutral country such as Sweden, which more than most others paid lip service to the internationalist peace logic, were secretly co-operating with Nato. The dominance of the realists, especially behind the scenes, effectively ensured that the European project did not assume political powers.

Yet, the greatest benefit for long term acceptance - and thereby political stability - was that the European project mission was quite straightforward, clearly understood by voters and neither much greater nor smaller than had been promised during the membership referendums. For this reason it enjoyed democratic legitimacy. However, with the fall of the Soviet Union, which proved to be a watershed moment also in the history of the European project, things changed fundamentally. As the security threat changed it was possible to afford, at least short term, not to be as 'boringly' realistic as before. The much more alluringly romantic internationalists, those who during the previous decades had been portrayed as 'lofty and naïve', found themselves in a position when *they* could assume control over the narrative. Increasingly the realist heroes and 'doers' of the previous era - soldiers, industrialists and realist politicians and diplomats focusing on protecting national interests - were portrayed as 'warmongers', 'greedy' or 'old-fashioned'. For the first time since the 1930s the internationalist mindset started to be used not only to seduce voters; it started to be *genuinely* believed among many European heads of government. The heroes of the new era soon proved to be the idealist wordsmiths such as academics, even students as well as the politicians and diplomats pushing the supposedly 'altruistic' supranational agenda.

Consequently the previous ideological division between the European federalists and member state governments dissolved. Instead of providing a counterweight to the federalist agenda many member state public servants started to actively *support* it. It did not take long until the European project transformed from an economics project (the EC) into a much more political project (the EU). This development was much encouraged by the repositioning of the major political parties towards the centre ground. Before that they had taken turns in the national parliaments to provide a counterweight to the continuous EU expansion plans. (Labour had offered fierce resistance as long they had suspected the EC to be a free trade 'capitalist' project. Small government Thatcherites offered fierce resistance after having been effectively outmanoeuvred over the social chapter introduced by socialists Mitterand and Jacques Delors, the starting point towards plenty of EU intervention of a much more political nature.)

Suddenly there was no strong force in national parliaments left that did provide a strong counterweight to the European project. Certainly, some people on the fringes grumbled but as long as the economy was booming these people were easy to outplay. It is no coincidence that the transformation of the EC from a mainly economic project to a totally different beast took place between the fall of the Soviet Union and the first major economic downturn thereafter. This could be dubbed 'the era of idealism unleashed'. When things started to look problematic again, after the 2007 economic dive and the 2015 commencement of Russian military interventionism, there was yet again greater scope for realism but by that time the internationalist school of thought was so deeply entrenched that many opinion makers had forgotten that it was not really based on realities on the ground but on the need for a politically convenient moral alibi.

Of course, all those who have invested considerable amounts of prestige in the internationalist peace paradigm, had no interest in refreshing any memories. If many people believe that international membership organisations such as the EU (and the UN) actually do play a key role by advancing peace, then people belonging to such organisations will no doubt continue to be widely supported.

It would certainly be nice if the highly idealistic internationalist line of thinking was not at odds with how things actually work. Conflicts of interest do exist and many of them will never dissolve regardless of how much they are discussed. In fact, despite the *official* support for the internationalist 'open-dialogue-and-no-national-interest-approach', even today diplomats would unofficially be considered to do a bad job if they were not prepped to actively *advance* the interests of the country or organisation they represent. If they really did disregard the national interest they would swiftly be replaced by somebody else. If 'outplaying' diplomats from other countries they, and the governments they represent, would be praised for diplomatic cunning.

This is why important international settlements are *never* reached through 'open unbiased dialogue'. Instead, the large countries conclude horse trading deals *bilaterally* and then make the smaller countries tag along. Only if the outcome hangs in the balance do the smaller nations stand a chance of influencing the outcome. Then frantic negotiations often follow during which the bigger countries compete in accumulating the additional support necessary. Also these negotiations are primarily carried out bilaterally. The most persuasive arguments, the clinchers, tend to focus around some big power offer that benefits the smaller countries. At times of European crisis the decisive dialogues will, almost without exception, take place bilaterally between the prime ministers, finance ministers or foreign ministers of Germany, France and the UK. When it is time for official discussion and voting in the actual meeting rooms the outcome is almost always a foregone conclusion.

It is outright dangerous to believe that the EU – or any other international organisation – has fundamentally refined or even altered the prerequisites for how decisions on defence policy are taken. Cunning old diplomats in the 19th century, individuals like Talleyrand or Metternich, would have, given fewer tassels on their clothes, felt well at home during the EU's (corridor) defence policy discussions. The only major difference would be that these, when subsequently facing the people and explaining why the talks had been enormously successful, would have had to replace the nationalist platitudes with platitudes signalling Pan European patriotism.

Given certain circumstances war *can* no doubt be avoided through a policy of appeasement. This is the case if potential enemies are really driven by fear of attack and if there is a risk that they will attack in order to forestall an expected attack. A familiar example is how the mobilisation of Russian and German troops, just before the outbreak of World War One, really might have affected the psychology leading to war.

However, given certain circumstances the 'hawkish' stance might prevent war. The most notorious example is of course how Hitler played the internationalist appeasers for fools. As pointed out by numerous people, had he met fiercer resistance after having occupied both Austria and Sudetenland he might never have attempted to invade Poland.

No elaborate academic construct is needed to make either point. Both can be made by consulting the school of the totally obvious. It is arguably equally obvious that it is nothing less than immensely dangerous – and thereby certainly irresponsible - to apply either the 'hawkish' or 'dovish' line of thinking to *all* circumstances.

It is also noteworthy that the EU federalist communication concerning Nato is marked by contradiction. The federalists often argue that the EU should provide a counterweight to Nato. The reasoning then typically goes that the USA is too dominant a member at the Nato table. The EU should therefore develop its own defence association.

However, when discussing *EU membership*, the EU integrationists typically claim that a seat at the table guarantees influence. Protestors about a certain EU policy are typically urged to stop muttering and to exploit their seat so as to influence the agenda. But if that line of reasoning holds, why then should the EU countries (most of them members of Nato) develop their own defence association? Why should the European Nato members not exploit their *many* seats at the Nato table?

If on the other hand it is really true that it can be difficult to influence the major actors in an international membership organisation, why should small countries like Sweden, Portugal and Bulgaria sit at the same European negotiating table as Europe's great powers, the UK, France and Germany? Would that not mean that Finnish, Swedish, Portuguese and Bulgarian defence policy would in practice be influenced by, amongst others, commercial agreements concluded between the real power players, for example gas pipeline agreements between Germany and Russia?

Moreover, the military lead of the USA is so immense – even when compared to the combined military powers of all EU member states - that it in all events holds most of the defence policy levers. As a consequence, is it not in the interest of the European people to accept this fact and to sit at the same table as the USA - even if for no other reason than for inclusion in the American defence shield? A change in that attitude would be rational if the individual EU member states were trying to bridge the defence capability gap. As it is, due to the defence cuts in Europe over recent years, that gap is *widening*.

It is not particularly difficult to conclude that the lofty peace logic underpinning the EU foreign policy service is a far cry from the realistic – and economically focused - peace logic that underpinned the original European project. In fact, it is easy to argue that the original peace logic has been distorted *to make room for the EU diplomatic service* and not the future stability of Europe.

When discussing matters of war and peace it is also useful to keep in mind that wars rarely or never start by attempts to maintain borders already well established. Instead, they typically start when 'visionaries' try to enforce new grander frontiers and position themselves at the top of the new power pyramid. And who is it that presently attempts to do precisely that in Europe?

*

2.6 Immigration debate bias

The ultimate reason the immigration issue is such an attention grabber is that net migration to the rich EU countries has reached levels that lack precedent. In the beginning of the 1990s net migration to the UK stood at around 40,000. Since 1997 that figure has risen significantly. In 2014 net migration was 318,000 of which 178,000 migrants arrived from other EU countries.[3031] There was another statistically significant rise in net migration after the Eastern European EU enlargement in 2004. However, even if leaving out internal EU migration net migration has clearly risen. Since the trend is general it suggests that many people migrating from other EU countries might have done so - and been allowed to do so - even if not having been part of the EU. However, it is also clear that the EU federalists have severely underestimated how many people, both within and outside the EU, would leave their home countries for richer pastures if the possibility was offered.

When strong passion enters a political debate hidden interests are usually involved. Many of those are certainly to be found also when scrutinising the immigration issue.

One factor of great importance to the *opponents* of large scale immigration is that the majority of immigrants who change countries without having employment arranged beforehand are of working age and without university education. This means tougher job competition in the receiving countries, especially in sectors employing low skilled workers. For native job-seekers this dilemma is compounded by many immigrants having proven prepared to accept both lower wages and working conditions below domestic standards.

Another factor, arguably severely underestimated, relates to relationship dynamics. Addition of new people, foreign or not, always affects the relationship dynamics and thereby also the power balance wherever the newcomers end up (workplaces, schools, football clubs, churches..).

Indeed, the relationship dynamic can be upset only by people moving in from the neighbouring village. If 1,000 unemployed Brits were to be forcibly relocated from London to York there would no doubt be resentment among people already living in York. However, resentment would be even greater if 1,000 unemployed people from Romania were forcibly placed in York. Why? Simply because people with different languages and cultures are more difficult to understand and engage with.

Addition of large numbers can change the overall relationship dynamics and power balance of an entire community, especially if a majority of the newcomers tend to be partial to one political party or to one religion. It would be totally unrealistic not to expect misunderstandings, power tests, uncertainty and the stress that follows from uncertainty.

The people who might lose out the most when newcomers arrive in a community – either in terms of tougher job competition or weaker (formal or informal) social standing (the football club?) – can naturally be expected to offer the stoutest resistance.

It is questionable if this particular recipe for possible resentment is much influenced by the fact that immigrants who do not find a job might end up receiving benefits. The weight of the possible extra cost will, in practice, be paid by middle-income and high-income earners (taxpayers) who are less personally affected by immigration.

However, if immigration adds to the delivery burdens of schools and hospitals it might start personally affecting people higher up on the social ladder - even if rarely the high(est)-income earners who take the political decisions and sometimes also come across as totally oblivious to the practical effects on the ground.

These are arguably the main reasons many people resist the growing levels of net immigration. However, few will openly reveal a personal fear of losing out, that would look too self-interested and might also draw unwanted attention to a possible lack of professional or social competitiveness. The opposition arguments will therefore be more vague and sweeping.

The perhaps most common excuse tends to be passed on as 'cultural'. References might be made to a perceived threat to the indigenous life-style. There can no doubt be a degree of mental comfort if managing to preserve the well-known. If nothing changes there is no need to take in, digest and rationalise new information. On the other hand, challenges to the old ways can also be a source of revitalization. However, if numbers arrive at a scale that the shape of the whole community changes, and politicians continue the one-sided talk about the need to show 'tolerance', it will no doubt create irritation among not only natives but also among early immigrants who managed to integrate well but *subsequently* start to be treated with suspicion while the absence of balance and moderation stirs up a general anti-immigrant sentiment.

When migrants start coming in hundreds of thousands every year – integration will also pose considerable practical and economical challenges. Where to put everyone? Who should pay for their rents, food, schools, language courses and training programmes? How to avoid terrorist infiltration? If politicians go and stay woolly on the subject – instead of offering the clear quote compromises, border controls and leadership that such a situation calls for – then resentment will grow to a point when it will destabilise the entire political system. Notoriously, this is of course precisely what has happened in many of the richer European countries.

So what are the main motives behind the wooliness for years fuelled by the EU federalists? The by far most important reason is that clear migration quotas would limit the 'freedom of movement' and seriously impede the federalist agenda of an ever deeper union. A constructive rather than nonsensical debate would also put into question the wisdom of having accepted countries like Romania and Bulgaria as full EU members; despite the fact that the economies and living standards of those countries were violating the (previous) EU rules.

These are the main reason the EU federalists have, for years, chosen to play the racist card whenever objections have been raised.

When exploiting the racist card the concept of 'virtue signalling' is also brought into play.[32] Virtue signalling takes place when a person wants to manifest *personal* virtue by communicating an emotionally loaded view which happens to be in vogue among those establishing the norm - and thereby also establish what is regarded as 'politically correct'. If and when this happens the debate has degenerated into focusing on the self-righteousness of the debaters.

If surprise follows from a failure to shame the sympathisers of the parties of discontent into submission it illustrates that the federalists are indeed acting in good faith – and also that they are completely out of touch with realities on the ground. Those having vented serious concerns about the parties of discontent will, not without reason, feel not only misunderstood but also neglected and offended. And they will have a nagging suspicion – rightly or wrongly - that the politically correct 'establishment politicians' have *deliberately* used them as scapegoats for personal mistakes.

However, an element of unawareness really might affect the views and rhetoric of the EU federalists. If you are an EU career federalist you typically earn many times more than the average earner and you also benefit from private healthcare and private schools. Given that most time is spent in the public servant halls of Europe, luxury hotels and restaurants and in gated communities you might rarely experience the practical consequences of mass migration. Your personal remunerations, allowances and pensions are certainly not affected. However, all can be lost if admitting major mistakes in the narrative. Someone else might then be able to take your place. And, after all, how can you be mistaken when you belong to the enlightened set of people who have read several major textbooks about internationalism, multiculturalism and open borders and when you have always stayed abreast by reading newspapers and magazines which in a similar way serve as de facto mouthpieces for the internationalist and multiculturalist mindset? With all these sources you will have been made aware, for sure, that in the long run migration benefits everyone. The disgruntled are clearly racists, how could it be otherwise!

With positions locked it is not really possible to constructively discuss which policies really help to ease the toils of either immigrants or concerned natives.

The racist cries are surely vastly exaggerated. Few mention that *for the first time in history* it is political suicide for any potential head of government to utter anything that could be even vaguely interpreted as down putting to foreigners. Equally few mention that the still existing *real* racists tend to be marginal figures on the fringes of society and that their attitude presumably to a great extent is based on a personal craving to be seen at least in some way. Compare the political influence of such more or less damaged individuals with the influence exercised by the people in power of the EU. Then it is not particularly difficult to conclude which 'forces' are, *in reality*, more potentially dangerous. It is almost as easy to conclude that no parties of discontent have the opportunity to win *real* government influence without first becoming more 'housetrained'.

Except, and this is an important exception, if the establishment parties across Europe continue to duck the tough but necessary decisions. People in less cherished sectors and in communities that are forced to absorb ever greater immigration numbers have expressed deep concerns not over immigration per se but over immigration numbers that have proven hard to absorb. As long as politicians do not take these concerns seriously – or only offer backing through lip service - the parties of discontent will continue to thrive and could possibly even make inroads *by escalating rather than moderating the narrative*.

The migration issue does bring talk of 'solidarity' with vulnerable people in the home country into conflict with talk of solidarity with vulnerable people in other member states. This suggests that anyone who takes side categorically have not really understood – or does not want to understand - the problem. It also suggests that the most constructive way ahead is to crunch the numbers and maintain a realistic focus. During times of economic uncertainty and unemployment, how many net immigrants enter and how many immigrants is it possible to accept, without unreasonably increasing the suffering among already domestic job seekers? Without upsetting the balance of communities excessively? Without risking the stability of the entire political system? Should funds, including additional development aid, be refocused to make things more economically bearable in countries from which migrants are leaving in great numbers?

Following the path of compromise would certainly not be rocket science, only good old political compromise. That is and always has been the only way to diffuse a sensitive political issue when emotions are strong and forces clash.

Yes, migration has to be allowed for all sorts of reasons, above all humanitarian reasons. Yes, for both theoretical and very practical reasons the concept of totally open borders has to be scrapped: in theory it has always been based on wishful thinking rather than scientific research and in practice it simply does not work.

The EU federalist refusal to accept compromise that affects its centralisation agenda serves no-one. In fact, given the political backlash, it now even endangers the integrationist agenda. When the EU federalists, in September 2015, imposed mandatory asylum seeker quotas on EU member countries they managed yet again to further extend the powers of Brussels.[33] Perhaps people already persuaded by the EU federalist narrative found this a sensible course of action. However, it created a political rift with several Eastern European member states. Moreover, many previously undecided voters also in other EU countries found the EU course of action unreasonable. This in turn suggests that the EU federalists, highly uncharacteristically, is losing even the tactical battle when it comes to immigration, and for good reason. The migration issue has been mishandled in a major way and underlines perhaps more strongly than anything else how politically dangerous it is when politicians are consumed by lofty idealism. It is this idealism that explains the scale of the political arrogance – because arrogance it is. The people of Europe – voters - have proven more tolerant than ever and are far better positioned than most politicians to understand what aspects need to be balanced to make the necessary compromises. Still the EU federalists have kept asking for more while distorting facts and treating voters as children who cannot handle the truth. As always the EU integrationist mission has been prioritised above everything else.

*

2.7 Biases linked to regional grants and subsidies

Around 40 percent of the EU budget is dedicated to agricultural subsidies and around 45 percent to 'regional and cohesion support'.[34] The latter includes grants and subsidies aiming to improve the economic conditions of the less affluent regions of Europe. Using the lion's share of EU money in this way explains why markedly industrialised EU member countries - such as Germany, the UK, the Netherlands and Sweden - are net contributors to the EU budget whilst countries with regions that are less affluent - such as Poland, Greece, Spain, Portugal, Romania, Bulgaria and Greece - are net recipients. That (the wine producer) France's governments defend the protectionist agricultural policy with tooth and claw – irrespective of the political colour of the government – is the result not so much of the relative financial size of the agricultural sector as the fact that the number of voters employed in the agricultural sector is still considerable (and vocal) in an electoral context. As a consequence France continues to be the politically strongest defender of the CAP (and the largest receiver of CAP money) despite having turned into a big overall net contributor to the EU budget.

About 40 per cent of the EU budget is spent on various forms of agricultural subsidies. Most are "direct" subsidies, known as the "single farm payment". Originally these subsidies were linked to how much meat or crops farmers produced. However, that system created the infamous wine lakes and butter mountains of the 1980s – literally huge quantities of food wasted due to over-production. To move away from this, EU leaders decided to "decouple" farm subsidies from production, meaning that the subsidy would be paid out based on other criteria, primarily land ownership. So far so good: price distortion was reduced and over-production (sort of) ended, whilst farmers still received their subsidies. There were catches though. The single farm payment was supposed to be a temporary measure. However, the number of potential receivers of grants and subsidies was expanded and with it the interest group of landowners. This in turn served to entrench the CAP even further. By linking the subsidy to land, recipients of EU "farm subsidies" now include the Queen of England, the King of Sweden, various multinational firms but also golf clubs, luxury hotels and a whole swarm of other illustrious beneficiaries.[35]

In effect, EU farm subsidies have turned into income support for a random group of people, justified on basis of a series of confused, and at times, conflicting objectives. Perhaps most critically, by providing income support irrespective of whether any meaningful economic activity takes place on a farm, direct CAP subsidies often act as an outright disincentive for farmers to modernise – not least in Eastern Europe. This in turn locks in unviable business models and hurts Europe's competitiveness.

So why have all attempts to fundamentally reform CAP been crushed? A key answer is that the agricultural lobby group is amongst the most powerful in Brussels. It is telling that many members on the European Parliament's Agriculture Committee, which has a big say over the bloc's farm policy, are themselves farmers. Replace "Agriculture" with "financial services" and "farmer" with "banker", and you would have a scandal. What has happened however is that the EU federalists are trying to change the narrative rather than the substance. Small changes are made and talked up. The wording surrounding it is changed. Today CAP falls under the more general label of "Preservation and management of natural resources".[36]

The EU's farm policy also involves considerable agricultural tariffs on food-producing countries outside the EU (though not strictly falling under CAP). This means that not only do taxpayers – who are also consumers – need to foot the bill for the subsidies; taxpayers also need to pay higher food prices than otherwise necessary. This means that taxpayers also, even if unknowingly, are limiting the opportunity of farmers in many poor (African) countries to exploit *their* unique competitive advantages – a lot of sun, low pay – in order to sell agricultural produce in one of the areas of the world with the greatest spending power, the European Union. If really caring about helping underdeveloped countries it is worth bearing in mind that no countries (except oil producing countries) have improved their living standards without first developing their agricultural sector. A complicating factor is that these tariff revenues, somewhat obscurely labelled 'Traditional own resources', make up more than 10 percent of total EU revenues.

The rationale for the structural and cohesion funds is in a way sound – public investment for economies that are "transitioning" from closed to open. Such funds can have a positive impact in individual cases if combined with good public administration and pro-growth policies. Perhaps not without merit the EU federalists like to present Ireland in the 1990s as a shining example.[37] Then again, during times of other big Irish developments in Ireland it is hard to determine how big of an effect the EU money actually made; Ireland substantially lowered its corporate tax burden, US direct investment was pouring in and all trading partners of Ireland experienced strong growth.

However, as with the CAP there are a number of problems. These problems would arguably be addressed if the key objective really was to achieve maximum value for money for society as a whole. Most fundamentally, currently all 28 EU countries take part in the structural funds, meaning that some of the richest countries on the planet – Germany, Sweden, the UK, the Netherlands, Denmark – effectively recycle money amongst themselves, via Brussels, to pay for each other's regional policy. This is wholly economically irrational. The European Commission has itself admitted that such a recycle exercise creates "considerable administrative and opportunity costs".[38]

Worse than that, centralising the power to distribute such a vast money pot, €70 bn, (another €60 bn for CAP purposes),[39] builds in several moral hazards. The reason is that it creates a structure which rewards people who are adept at playing the bureaucratic system. This in turn encourages a climate of lobbying and cosying up 'to the right people'. It is no coincidence that lobbying towards EU politicians and civil servants is nowadays an integral part of EU operations. This means that well organised interest groups (typically producers) gain on behalf of groups less organised (consumers and taxpayers).[40]

Even during the days of the Roman empire it was basic knowledge that when the ultimate power is far, far away it creates, in practice, an incentive structure that fosters the creation of Potemkin villages built with the prime purpose of obtaining grants. Both regional public sector project plans and private sector business plans are often heavily skewed in ways meant to make them appealing to the EU bureaucrats deciding grants – while sometimes making them out of touch with realities on the ground.

It is not unusual, neither should it be surprising, that playing the budget game is a main activity, sometimes even *the* main activity, of many ventures which seek EU money earmarked for regional development.

There are other closely related moral hazards. MPs are often punished at the ballot box if non-profitable businesses with many employees are closed in their constituencies – even if the long term prospects of these businesses is unviable. EU funds can keep alive uncompetitive industries or be used to start new political prestige projects. In the UK, Welsh politicians, for example, are amongst the keenest on "EU money", despite no clear evidence that these funds have made an overall positive impact in Wales. Similarly, there is a great risk that the EU federalists are exploiting the power of the purse to reward "EU friendly" ventures, thereby buying regional support.

A moral hazard on the government level, also a direct consequence of money being sent to the EU only to be sent back, is that many EU countries – including net contributors such as the UK – are often more concerned about claiming "victory" over how much money it manages to claw back, rather than focusing on if the money is well spent.

Under the current structure it would actually be surprising if public money was *not* frequently channelled away from where it can be well spent. Think tank Open Europe used to produce a yearly list over wasteful projects (already referred to in a note above).[41]

Example of money wasted: The Iberian Peninsula has seen the construction of a whole range of underused "ghost" roads, airports and harbours – funded by taxpayers across Europe. Possibly around 25 per cent of the structural funds in Portugal have been invested in roads, heavily contributing to a strange situation where the country has 60 per cent more kilometres of motorway per inhabitant than Germany and four times more than Britain – but with little corresponding demand. Meanwhile, around a third of the EU structural funds ending up in Spain between 2007 and 2013 was invested in infrastructure, thereby intensifying an already massive construction bubble. When it burst it sent the country into an economic crisis. The EU's own auditors have criticised EU spending on roads, noting that 74 per cent of the project they monitored recorded less traffic than expected.[42]

"Cohesion policy is definitely a policy we can be proud of and continue to be proud of in the future. We need to be strong and clear in promoting this position."[43] (José Barroso)

The *need* for lobbying and politicking is now an integral part of the EU system. Beneficiaries are highly concentrated to a series of small, strongly organised groups. Those paying the price are spread out across groups that naturally are poorly organised: taxpayers, consumers, budding entrepreneurs not in tune with the public sector mindset as well as the unemployed who never get the chance to work in ventures that *could* have been realised.

The criticism presented certainly does not mean new ventures should not be supported in areas with high unemployment. Neither does it rule out a strong social safety net. However, it does mean that grant and subsidy decisions should be brought closer to home.

Taking budget decisions closer to the regions would save administrative costs by, beneficially, cutting the number of middlemen involved. It would also help to reduce the sometimes long stretches of partly unproductive 'gap periods' - when things come close to a standstill while ventures are waiting for the budget decisions. Most crucially, ensuring that civil servants involved have at least one ear to the ground is crucial if really striving to grasp which ventures add long term value and which do not.

Arguably, if there *is ever* a need to apply the subsidiarity principle it is when handing out grants and subsidies aiming to reinvent regional economies. However, it is also easy to argue that it could have made sense to decentralise the power of the purse from the member state capitals to the regions. The EU federalists made sure that the very opposite happened. There should be little doubt that a key motive has been to wield the tremendous political powers linked to the money pots discussed. Indeed, the quest for money has in a sense created another industry, an EU grant-and-subsidy-seeking-industry, but this service industry is of questionable value to society. It is propped up by numerous players who, often because of career interests, sing from the same hymn sheet: public sector administrators, lobbyists, MPs fishing for easy votes as well as an armada of EU PR-campaigners[44]. To make it all sound better regional subsidies are now sorted under the budget heading 'Smart and inclusive growth'.[45]

There is no need to make ideological standpoints over this. Public sphere meddling can be useful. Misguided public sphere meddling is not. It is far from the first time in history that bureaucrats have tried to orchestrate economic growth from the top. Then as now wishful political thinking has too often triumphed over realities on the ground. Many of the regions that have received 'help' from the EU structural and cohesion funds had probably been much better off if decision making had returned to the national level. The same goes for taxpayers paying for the money circus.

*

2.8 Biases of freedom from responsibility and lobbying

Another conflict of interest arises while it is sometimes practically easier for a member state government to pass legislation within the EU legislative apparatus than within its own. The *national* process of legislation always requires drafting and battling in parliamentary committees. If the proposal discussed is important politicians from the opposite camp(s) most often offer resistance in the traditional – fierce - sense. The process and battle lines are then hard to conceal, not least while politicians involved are national figures which attract lots of interest and attention. Also, many documents and minutes are made public. Moreover, politicians involved frequently use media leaks as a bargaining tool. As a consequence, it is close to impossible for a national government to work on a controversial piece of legislation and avoid tough counter-attacks from both other parties and from journalists.

In *the EU's legislative process* 'difficulties' of this kind are much easier to avoid. This is to a great extent a result of a much more limited insight into EU activities, not least while common to classify discussions and documents as secret. Most civil servants will also have been forbidden to speak to journalists or researchers about anything sensitive. Even if and when an interesting comment can be retrieved from Mr-or-Mrs-Influential-Foreigner it might still not sell papers nationally since no-one really knows who it is. When the handful of famous EU representatives speak their appearances are usually carefully choreographed. The same goes for all major texts produced by the EU apparatus. As a consequence correspondents and researchers will have only skewed data at their disposal.

The insight into the EU machinery is also reduced by a lower general understanding of the EU colossus. Which officials within a General-Directorate are practically influential and which are not? Which commissioners are push-overs and which are not? Which lobbyists have influenced the political agenda and which have not? Also the broad sharing of responsibilities between EU institutions and agencies creates problems. By referring to someone else it is a piece of cake to leave journalists and other possible inquirers empty-handed.

The EU moreover offers a sort of freedom from responsibility for national politicians. If the decisions that are carried through the EU apparatus prove popular, then it is possible to claim that the personal contribution made a major impact. This will not be gainsaid on the international scene; all other Heads of Government will say the same on their respective home turf. If on the other hand the decisions prove unpopular, national politicians can express a mumbling EU critique and say that, in an organisation with many members, you do not always get what you want.

Another key aspect is that national politicians who pick a fight with the Brussels machinery have much to lose. Such a fight could, in particular, mean a loss of international allies and thereby deteriorating prospects of policy collusion (promoting each other's agendas) when advancing causes that really are considered important in the home country. For national politicians there are therefore strong incentives, when dealing with international organisations, to choose the battles carefully and, most of the time, just play along.

These factors explain why there is most often a much stronger bipartisan understanding within the EU legislative apparatus than within a national legislative apparatus.

On the national scene, where they are being watched, politicians need to fight fierce battles in order to position themselves. On the supranational scene, where they are not much watched at all, they ensure that it remains that way by colluding and by *not* pointing out each other's mistakes and flaws.

As a consequence, getting laws through the EU apparatus can be more or less a formality, due to the fact that almost all of Europe's governments have for years had a clear centrist, - EU embracing -

character this has happened regularly - even with major pieces of legislation.

These factors explain why there is limited opportunity to get an insight into what happens in Brussels. Life as a politician is simply made so much easier when not having to face as much scrutiny as on the national level. It also leaves the door wide open to the intense public servant lobbyism and backroom quid pro quo (horse trading and policy collusion) agreements which often are concluded unofficially and *really* determine EU decisions.

Given a realistic perspective there is also much to be said about lobbyism which is carried out with the purpose of gaining special favours from legislators. Favours could come in the form of laws skewed to the specific benefit of the lobby group interest while at the cost of groups less well organised (including the public). Favours could also mean lucrative government contracts (in the private sector) or public sphere budget increases, grants or other types of subsidies. There is indeed a risk that lots of money is 'wasted' when lobby groups compete for favours[46]. If a lobby group in the private sphere stands a good chance of actually gaining the favour it might spend almost as much money as the contract is worth. Public sector lobbyists competing for government funds, including many directors of government sponsored agencies and NGOs, might focus their entire operation towards ticking the right boxes rather than providing the service which is the actual raison d'etre of their organisation.

Billions of euros are, *every day*, turned around in the EU system. The personal effect for bureaucrats, if the money is ill-spent, is small. Why? Because the costs are assumed by the general public and, due to the lack of transparency, the likelihood that someone will be able to categorically 'prove' it was ill-spent is also small. For these inverted reasons the incentive is much greater to either not care, or to spend the money in ways that boosts a personal agenda. For example by spending it on political prestige projects, on projects that due to political convenience help to boost next year's budget, on 'information campaigns' that boosts the image of the EU or on projects or investigations that carry (lobbyist) favours in return.

Many outsiders do not stand much of a chance of knowing about the dealings between, on the one hand, EU politicians and civil servants, and on the other, lobbyists. It should come as no great surprise that a vast amount of lobbyists, possibly about 15,000 private lobbyists, attempt to influence the EU's institutions in Brussels. The total number of EU lobbyists, including those from other governmental and non-governmental organizations, has been estimated at 55,000.[47]

It should come as no big surprise that most well-capitalised organisations both within the private and public sector (including trade unions), that have the clout to make lobbying efforts count, have transformed into staunch EU supporters. This has further legitimised the EU, meaning that everyone directly involved benefits. It also means that few if any mention it as a problem. In fact, one of EU's many open secrets is how Brussels, just like Washington, has transformed into a lobbyist Mecca.

Neither should it come as a great surprise that power centralisation breeds corruption.[48] Forms of corruption include not only underhanded lobbyism but also, amongst others, nepotism and 'disappearance' of taxpayer money. Every year there is, referring to the latter, controversy while the EU auditors point to considerable sums of money that are not properly accounted for. When someone mentions this 'inconvenient' circumstance, typically some EU politician at the middle management level is brought forward to shake his or her head while promising to do better next time, before quickly switching to talking about corruption within member states. This process has more or less turned into a yearly ritual.

When the EU commission was at last pressured to do something more, in 2012, it promised a major corruption investigation in order to study corruption *both* in individual member states and within the EU. The person responsible for the investigation was Sweden's Cecilia Malmström, then Commissioner for Home Affairs.

When the report was eventually published, in February 2014, after two years of investigation, it appeared that only corruption in individual member states had been investigated.[49] Malmström was keen to talk about that sort of corruption but was silent about not having, despite promises, also looked into corruption within the EU. Her spokesman communicated that internal scrutiny had proven difficult to carry out. The matter would be dealt with in a 'future' corruption report.[50]

If someone feels tempted to break the cosy consensus it risks coming at a great personal cost, as experienced by the harsh treatment of whistleblowers. This includes, to name but three: Marta Andreasen (an EU chief auditor who was suspended after refusing to sign accounts she found unreliable[51]), Dorte Schmidt-Brown (an EU chief accountant who was dismissed after highlighting possible malpractices at Eurostat[52]) and Paul van Buitenen (auditor at the European Commission who was suspended after highlighting particular cases of cronyism and possible corruption[53]).[54]

The consequences for economist Bernard Connolly were perhaps less surprising while he aired his EU criticism externally. While Head of the Affairs at the European Commission he wrote and published a book which was highly critical of both the intent and design of the Monetary Union. For arguably speaking many important truths he was not only sacked (in 1995), six years later the European Court of Justice ruled in favour of the sacking. The Court simultaneously set a legal precedent for outlawing EU employee criticism of EU institutions.[55]

The EU institutions have moreover been criticised for neutralising 'dissidents' by using psychologists to classify them as mentally unstable - tests orchestrated by compliant human resource departments.[56]

Also people external to the EU might need to be careful before presenting criticism. Hans-Martin Tillack, a then Stern reporter who was investigating irregularities linked to both Eurostat and OLAF (the European anti-fraud office), was arrested by Belgian police after OLAF officials alleged that Tillack had used bribes to obtain his information. His house and office were searched and documents, computers and telephones were seized. In 2005 the European Court of Justice ruled in favour of forcing Hans-Martin Tillack to reveal his sources to the European Commission.[57] Tillack appealed to the European Court of Human Rights (a non-EU institution) which in 2007 ruled in Tillack's favour while declaring that journalists must be able to protect the identity of their sources, and also that the claims against Tillack were based on "vague and unsustained rumors". The spokesperson for the European Commission said that Belgium had been found at fault rather than the EU institutions.[58]

Indeed, as long as an organisation is sufficiently powerful to suppress news of most scandals — and the internal reactions to them - harsh treatment might be what it takes to preserve the status quo and thereby fully in line with the self-interest of EU officials. As researched by Economics professors Manfred J. Holler and Bengt-Arne Wickström:

"On the battle ground of scandals, the strategy of "do not take prisoners" corresponds to warning fellow players not to respond to a scandal by choosing a strategy which is different from the status quo - because if you do so, you will never again achieve a preferred position and you endanger the favorable position of those fellow players who are not threatened by a scandal. This explains, at least to some extent, why fellow players often queue up to help sweeping scandals under the carpet."[59]

*

2.9 Academic bias

Another significant conflict of interest leads into the academic world. In all ages there has been a strong link between the typical political colour of the academic output and the dominating political colour in parliament. The reason is a simple one; the government and parliament decides most university budgets and usually also exercises the ultimate power of appointment.

This explains why it was necessary to look very hard, during the pre-democratic era, to find anything but right-wing professors of social science. For decades before and after the democratic breakthrough, it was by turns progressive social liberals or progressive (Fabian) social democrats who dominated the academic scene (depending on who formed the government). Prominent examples include Sidney and Beatrice Webb, John Maynard Keynes and William Beveridge. In the 1960s the left-wing factions of many Labour parties managed to gain the upper hand. From then on and a few decades onwards the academic scene was heavily influenced by those providing a moral alibi for the 'radical left', people like Jean Paul Sartre and Simone de Beauvoir. Temporarily, during the era of Reagan and Thatcher, it was the academic antithesis, Milton Friedman, who was offered superhero status. At present, when the political centre ground is more dominant than ever, we are back to a period when social science professors adhering to *progressive* views are given the by far greatest scope. This explains the current star status given to social liberal interventionists such as Paul Krugman, Joseph Stiglitz and Christopher Pissarides. This also includes many of Europe's presently most hailed philosophers, people like Jacques Derrida and Jürgen Habermas. The *reasoning* leading up to the conclusions of such academics vary, depending not only on which direction they are coming from but also on individual levels of creativity. However, it is very rare to find any of them reach conclusions that are useful to anything but the progressive internationalist camp.

Given that empirical evidence supposedly should be the cornerstone of an academic debate it is somewhat ironic that many such academics appear to be much less concerned about realities on the ground than how they *want* reality to look. A common denominator when academic research is heavily politicised is that when evidence does not fit into the preferred line of thinking it is simply ignored. Academics closely connected with *abstract idealism*, thinkers such as Plato, Immanuel Kant, Woodrow Wilson, Jürgen Habermas and Jacques Derrida, do however even provide explicit justification for skipping empirical fieldwork. All these share the view that ideas tend to control reality rather than the other way around. Consequently, if things do not work well on the ground improvement efforts should be focused on freely contemplating how things *should* be rather than proceed from how things actually are.

Jacques Derrida and Jürgen Habermas in a widely published co-written book chapter/article:[60]

"We welcome the Europe that found exemplary solutions for two problems during the second half of the twentieth century. The EU already offers itself as a form of governance beyond the nation-state, which could set a precedent in the post national constellation. And for decades, European social welfare systems served as a model. Certainly, they have now been thrown on the defensive at the level of the national state. Yet future political efforts at the domestication of global capitalism must not fall below the standards of social justice that they established. If Europe has solved two problems of this magnitude, why shouldn't it issue a further challenge: to defend and promote a cosmopolitan order on the basis of international law against competing visions?"

"A bellicose past once entangled all European nations in bloody conflicts. They drew a conclusion from that military and spiritual mobilization against one another: the imperative of developing new, supranational forms of cooperation after the Second World War. The successful history of the European Union may have confirmed

Europeans in their belief that the domestication of state power demands a mutual limitation of sovereignty, on the global as well as the national-state level."

It is no coincidence that the internationalist strand of thinking is permeated not only by a progressive bias but also an abstract rather than a so called realist thought pattern. Few internationalists would perhaps openly admit a disregard for fieldwork, if and when doing so it invites the criticism of being out of touch. However, there should be little doubt that some academics, including just about every (EU) internationalist, have a more 'relaxed' attitude to the value of thorough and balanced fieldwork. The notion that it *is* possible to take international co-operation to a much higher level - through 'togetherness' - permeates every argument. If there is friction along the way, get back to the drawing table, the route chosen must then simply have been the wrong one. However, only 'cynics' waiver in their belief about the final destination.

To no small degree the EU clash is a clash between realists and idealists. The EU, built on the premise that human affairs can be much improved through fundamentally remodelling the political system, *needs* a great portion of idealist belief. Fieldwork is used to support the thesis, not question it.

Two American Presidents and two different views on the internationalist thinking leading to the League of Nations

"The age is an age... which rejects the standards of national selfishness that once governed the counsels of nations and demands that they shall give way to a new order of things in which the only questions will be: Is it right? Is it just? Is it in the interest of mankind?" President Woodrow Wilson

"I regard the Wilson-Bryan attitude of trusting to fantastic peace treaties, to impossible promises, to all kinds of scrap of paper without any backing in efficient force, as abhorrent... A milk-and-water righteousness unbacked by force is to the full as wicked as and even more mischievous than force divorced from righteousness." President Theodore Roosevelt

This certainly does not mean that *all* research conducted by today's political scientists has an idealist and progressive bias. It does however mean that academics who offer lines of reasoning well in sync with such thinking, while politically convenient, are the ones most often noticed and published.

As indeed always before there is an intimate win-win relationship between politicians and academics. The academics that make the proper EU noises are promoted to 'EU experts' and are offered additional funding, seats on expert committees as well as prizes and book contracts. The experts then repay the favours by lending legitimacy to the EU project and also by acting as academic gatekeepers against conflicting views. How? Not least by controlling the peer review process which most often decide if an academic article or book is to be published. Look for "EU politics series" (or similar) and there will most often – even if the publisher is *organisationally* independent – be links to universities, research institutes and referees that are heavily funded by the EU. Titles published within such a context are every year spitted out in hundreds and the vast majority of them are well in sync with the EU federalist narrative (and certainly not with a public choice perspective unless, possibly, heavily twisted). Those new titles immediately expand the body of "up to date EU research" which the next writer needs to pay heed to if counting on a warm reception by the gatekeepers.

To no small degree the EU clash is a clash between, just so, realists and idealists. The exceptions are as remarkable as they are few. Professor Roland Vaubel, who has explicitly researched the vested interests and centralisation bias within the four major EU institutions - the Commission, The Council, The Parliament and the European Court of Justice - is a notable example[61]. Professor Patrick Minford is another. When dissecting the conventional EU narratives in an EU book published in 2005 he was already famous for challenging academic mainstream thinking.[62][63]

To the extent other academics have had the integrity to investigate the EU from a genuinely critical perspective there is reason to suspect many might not have prevailed in the peer review publication process to the extent they might deserve.

All this means that academics specialising on the EU who take the call for impartiality and truth seeking seriously will always also be seriously disadvantaged. If not giving up altogether – and just start going with the flow – it means struggling on away from the limelight. Numerous (handpicked) academics have indeed given theoretical approval of more or less every step taken since the EC transformed into the EU. There have also been many admirable academics who have offered objective and constructive critique. Unsurprisingly their objections have been dismissed or not even considered in political circles.

The cycle created is self-perpetuating. Real critics will be so few they are easy to dismiss as outliers. "Surely you can see that the overwhelming body of academic evidence is pointing in a supportive direction."

There is certainly a strong correspondence between academic conclusions politically useful to the EU federalists and the most typical findings of 'distinguished' EU academics. In fact, the correspondence is so strong that it can easily, given that the supposed task of an academic is to offer a rounded view, be described as nothing less than ludicrously unscientific. However, due to the closed nature of the (eco)system in which politicians and academics relate to each other, this has proved to be of little importance. Taxpayers who are compelled to pick up the tab are dispersed, unorganised and usually unaware. This means that the 'academic show' can carry on quite undisturbed.

It was probably no coincidence that, when in February 2014 Barroso delivered a big parliamentary election speech in Great Britain, he chose to deliver it at the London School of Economics. The LSE has been a progressive bastion ever since the institution was founded in 1895 (by the socialist progressive legends Sidney and Beatrice Webb). The atmosphere was arguably good-humouredly paternalist when he gave his well-rehearsed address.[64] Uncomfortable EU criticisms were noticeable mainly by their absence, unless marked by straw man misrepresentation and then shot down with humorous sarcasm. Time after time Barroso assured his audience that greater EU integration is synonymous with a greater concern for the next generation. The spirit of his speech was difficult to mistake: Everything bad comes from obstinate member states and the banks, everything good from the EU. But have faith; there are really no major problems in the world that cannot be resolved if electors simply follow the 'EU-friendly' line of cooperation and integration. EU sceptics are nothing more than bitter reactionaries.

After Barroso's speech, Peter Sutherland, then Chairman of the *LSE*, gave a speech (also a former EU Commissioner). He described Barroso's speech as particularly constructive and claimed that it raised the entire level of British debate on the EU.

The only hint of criticism came from the moderator who claimed that the EU Commission at times was characterised by too much "classical liberal thinking". In this renowned bastion of learning no one mentioned that political power centralisation coupled with far-reaching intervention in key markets could be considered much more markedly progressive than anything else.

A month before Barroso delivered that speech, in January 2014, Christopher Pissarides delivered a public lecture at the London School of Economics (his academic home turf). As a British Cypriot and international academic heavyweight, Pissarides was a driving force when Cyprus controversially joined the euro. This did not prevent him from being awarded the Nobel Prize in Economics in 2010, despite the then ongoing Euro crisis. When the prize winner was determined it was presumably not unimportant that throughout the entire period of the crisis he had been and remains a strong voice in favour of *further* deepening of the EU project. Towards the end of Christopher Pissaride's LSE lecture he said this: "I was born a Keynesian and I will die a Keynesian. This is what gave me the Nobel Prize." Of course, telling humour often contains quite a lot of truth.

The bank of highly serviceable academics is continuously expanding. One of numerous examples is the 2014 winner of the Nobel Prize for Economics, Jean Tirole, professor at the Toulouse School of Economics. Tirole explicitly wants to add additional regulatory powers to the EU and he also wants additional EU-countries to be part of the eurozone. Moreover, he considers the EU budget small. In his view the EU should be given the mandate to oversee that northern Europe shares unemployment benefits and budgets with southern Europe.[65]

When the EU project is to be assessed by 'independent' experts, the task typically goes to people like Sutherland, Pissarides, Tirole - or one of their many fellow travellers. Just as intended, the overall grade, A+, is a foregone conclusion.

During more recent years, marked by economic downturn, there has been a fracture within the large team of politically useful academic EU supporters. Not surprisingly this crack has emerged over the politically sensitive issue of 'austerity'. As long as the EU institutions kept the floodgates of lending fully open to the Southern European spenders all was well in academic circles. Sending money from rich countries to somewhat less rich countries was fully in line with the current political bias.

However, when the economy dipped the international creditors, as previously discussed, turned uneasy. Would the Greeks really be able to honour their promises of debt repayment despite never ceasing to spend more money than was coming in from taxes and other sources of income? As ECB was the ultimate guarantor of these loans the EU taxpayers would have to foot the bill if the loans were not repaid. At long last the ECB (and IMF) declared that the Greek governments would have to impose 'austerity' measures in order to receive further loans, meaning that Greece would have to restructure its economy (including collecting more tax). The obvious purpose was to balance the budget so as to avoid being trapped in a debt spiral for decades. Since then many academics typically consulted by governments in (northern) European (net contributor) countries have advocated economic restraint as opposed to academics typically consulted by governments in (southern) European (net recipient) countries.

The involvement of academics also in these turn of events are arguably severely underestimated. With already huge amounts of debt it is questionable if the left-wing Syriza government (which the Greeks voted for in January 2015) would have dared to suggest the always most convenient remedy for unrelenting big spenders: spend even more - unless academics with a rockstar standing among progressives, people such as Krugman and Stiglitz, had provided academic (and moral) support while simultaneously splitting public opinion.[6667]

If a private company was funding a professor to assess the society usefulness of the company, nobody would believe in the impartiality of that professor. The fact that academics can get away with praising their paymasters - and still be hailed as impartial intellectuals - illustrates that the romanticism that surrounds politicians and civil servants extends also to the academic wedge of the public sphere.

In one sense it would still be wrong to conclude that the academic world is inherently skewed towards a progressive way of thinking. Before the introduction of democracy the bias was markedly right-wing. For a long time that right-wing bias certainly contributed to maintain suspicion about not only 'Labour revolutionaries' but also of progressives. It is truer to say that the academic world is inherently biased towards *any* strand of thinking which happens to dominate the public sphere paymasters. Which means that also when the political wind changes next time 'research' will yet again shift accordingly – even if with a time lag since entrenched thinking is rooted out only slowly.

*

2.10 Media bias

What, then about the fourth estate, the press? Do journalists keep a sharp eye on the political caste and call out when the narrative is heavily skewed, or when politicians fail to look out for domestic voter interests in international organisations? If it did member state public servants would not dare to be too meek during international negotiations as it might lead to voter punishment. The press would serve as the ultimate safeguard against system ill health setting in. After all, that is how it is supposed to be.

Unfortunately there is no guarantee this will happen, at least not an effective guarantee. Arguably there is often a heavy bias towards politicised thinking *both* within media corporations driven as for-profit-corporations and within public service media corporations; even if for different reasons.

Within *profit-driven* media corporations there is a strong commercial logic to fly the flag of one political camp. This has much to do with most readers and viewers tending to prefer media outlets confirming rather than challenging already adopted lines of thinking. As always, self-interest is part of the equation when picking the newspaper or news channel closest to your own political views. If you work in the public sector or are connected to a trade union you might be inclined to pick up the Guardian, as that is where you can expect to find strong support for a position benefitting you personally - not least moral support making you forget the self-interest. The inverted reasoning is true for many in the private sector who, for the very same reason, might pick up a right-wing paper. However, psychology also plays in. It is a lot easier, mentally to verify rather than challenge positions already held.

For obvious reasons also, advertisers prefer distinct profiles. In the UK large trade unions, typically EU friendly, advertise in the Guardian, often read by potential members. Large private corporations, typically EU friendly, advertise in the Financial Times, read by potential customers across the world. Advertisers wanting to reach a more EU sceptic audience, for example pensioners, can choose the Telegraph (the only large UK newspaper which gives just about equal weight to EU sceptics and EU supporters).

None of this necessarily means that political editors and political journalists need to 'prostitute' personal opinions. It does however mean that the owners who select editors – who in turn select which journalists to bring on board - choose among candidates with opinions in sync with the opinions that tend to please their typical readers and advertisers. Meaning that the reader or viewer collective, to a largely unconscious degree, shape 'their' media outlets more than the other way around. Also meaning that the job of political commentators, to a much higher degree than typically acknowledged, is to confirm and refine political preconceptions.

"All of us show bias when it comes to what information we take in. We typically focus on anything that agrees with the outcome we want." Noreena Hertz

Public service media corporations are more directly in tune with the political views dominating *in parliament* and thereby, by reflection, with the most typical views of voters (given a healthy state of the democracy). To a large degree this has, unsurprisingly, to do with the fact that government ministers typically nominate the executives of the national broadcasting corporations. In practice this more or less rules out everyone with a political profile distinctly different from the mainstream view. The choices will be passed on as apolitical while mainstream views, per definition, are less controversial than other views (and while the majority has always used its interpretation privileges to set the perception norms). However, now as always before the majority view in parliament will be just about as political as any other view – the main difference is rather that it will be more broadly supported.

Consequently it would actually be unreasonable to expect public service media corporations to act as anything but mouthpieces of mainstream political thinking. Today meaning social liberal – EU supportive – thinking.

There is another closely connected element that compounds the mainstream bias, an element that influences both journalists operating in the profit and the public service corporations. Since the parliamentary majority exercises budget and nomination powers in almost *all* pillars of society, journalists seeking people to interview will have a hard time finding top level experts who represent anything but the mainstream view.

Meaning in practice a journalist - after perhaps having interviewed a couple of academics, a couple of public sphere EU experts, a couple of civil servants, the heads of a couple of agencies and a couple of curators - might be convinced that he or she has acquired a well-rounded perspective; for example regarding staying or leaving within the EU. However, he or she might still have failed to find even one "person of authority" to offer anything but EU support. To find someone offering also a different perspective an interviewer might need to turn *outside* the public sphere. Then again, the journalists might not want to, or be quick themselves, to disregard alternative views and testimonies. Why? Public sphere romanticism – including EU romanticism - is likely to have been broadcasted in many of the (public sphere) schools and universities in which most journalists have been educated.

The political inclinations of leading commentators, in every EU country, might also be affected by the fact that the overwhelming majority tend to live in the capital and thereby in the stronghold of social liberal – 'EU friendly' - thinking. Some journalists might live and breathe the typically social liberal metro life and treat alternative lifestyles – and opinions - as something quaint, perhaps exotic but also outlandish, meaning the media understanding of the 'metro perspective' might be instantaneous, whilst it requires a considerably greater effort – and willpower – to genuinely understand the perspectives of people in different settings and situations. This helps to explain why national media is usually excellent at reflecting the majority mood within the capital but often less adept at hitting the mark when trying to portray the mood in other parts of a country.

There is also an element of risk-aversion. Standing out from the crowd is always associated with risk; this is rarely the case when following the herd. Who dares to challenge the institutionalised (centrist) experts in society – professors, internationalist Nobel Prize winners, Central Bank Presidents, 'independent' chairs of enquiries, the bulk part of prominent (centrist) commentators – when they are all singing pretty much the same

EU song? Over the last decade not many people have objected when writing yet another piece challenging 'EU-sceptics'. Instead, such pieces have typically been followed by lots of backslapping: "Yep, well said, you certainly make an important point!" However, challenge the wisdom of internationalism, the political bias of the academic sector or the independence of the European Central Bank and there is either dead silence or a number of people in authority explaining how misguided or even ridiculous you are. In earlier eras the defence arguments were directed elsewhere but the reaction pattern was strikingly similar.

The distance to Brussels and lack of insight and understanding of the complex EU machinery creates a bias problem specific to only the European project. In an ideal world Brussels correspondents would bridge the distance challenges. However, in practice there are no guarantees Brussels correspondents do not turn into a part of the problem. It is easy for EU public servants and press officers to offer special treatment to EU-friendly correspondents, for instance by offering longer and more frequent interviews as well as a greater number of invitations to wining and dining events. With time relationships easily turn semi-private, which goes hand-in-hand with friendly correspondents given a heads-up on certain news.

Just as intended it will appear, not totally without merit, as if those specially treated correspondents have a special insight into the corridors of power in Brussels. Nevertheless they will quickly be in line for the status as 'expert EU correspondents'. If *not* playing the 'game', meaning broadcasting the carefully orchestrated EU messages with at most a dash of criticism, for the sake of appearance, there is a risk someone who does play the game surpasses you to your position. Which means saying goodbye to international glamour, money and prestige, as well as buddy relationships with some of the most important men and women of our age.

The fact that many of Europe's most distinguished Brussels correspondents rarely or ever deviate much from the EU PR scripts illustrates that the proximity problem is real.

There is also a small country dimension which helps to explain why UK reformers have been struggling to find allies among EU member states even when these, on paper, might look like strong *potential* allies. Sweden provides a perfect example. Sweden is an export oriented country outside the Eurozone and also a net contributor to the EU budget: factors that all make the Swedish economy similar to the UK economy. It is also a country with a shifting political landscape largely due to the toxic immigration issue.

Due to numerous factors mentioned in this book it is quite possible to argue that Sweden would benefit immensely from EU downscaling. At minimum it would be reasonable to expect a serious EU debate, meaning a debate not only largely mimicking the narrative in Brussels. However, since Sweden joined the EU in 1995, not even one prominent Swedish media outlet has raised concerns that challenge the EU in a major way. Yes, a few remarks here and there about topical corruption scandals or the tactical handling of major events but nothing that *seriously* questions Swedish EU membership whereas EU sceptics are habitually treated with much sarcasm. Meaning that it arguably has been (and still is) impossible for Swedish readers and viewers to experience an honest presentation of the EU federalist counterarguments.

The lack of opinion diversity does not only relate to the EU; if one single term can generally describe the Swedish public debate it is, arguably, conformity. Why is that? A key answer is that in a country with a small population there is little commercial possibility for opinion camps deviating from the mainstream; the niche opinions.

Moreover, when a mindset has been institutionalised for decades, such as the internationalist mindset, few might even recognise its strong political subtext. As 'everyone' lends support to *the* opinion camp the general direction of a chosen course of action will never really be challenged. Not even flagrant overshooting will then necessarily be disputed. The climate of debate will be conformist to a degree that a 'rebel' will be perceived as only one of two things; either someone twisting a point or two in a minor way while posturing as if the difference is dramatic; or someone saying the same thing as everyone else but with a higher voice. People really standing out – those expressing truly different views - will either be rejected by all media outlets or immediately branded as eccentrics probably driven by devious motives. Against such people normal civility codes will not be necessary, meaning that sarcasm and highly personal attacks will often be used as weapons of demotion, which in turn makes it even more risky to be connected with the wrong ideas. It follows that demonstrating orthodoxy is then the only safe way to avert the risk of all risks: the marking out as a deviator. This explains why virtue signalling, arguably, has turned into a Swedish national sport, and why moral smugness, which always has been a close relative of a conformist opinion climate, is not cut down to size.

During seminar discussions over the health of Swedish journalism numerous people in authority – prominent editors and media professors – typically reach the conclusion that media objectivity has never been greater. Many who say such things will genuinely believe it to be true. After all, only oddballs say otherwise.

Moreover, while the small country conformity mechanisms are quite subtle these open the door to diplomatic misunderstandings. Ironically the arguably much superior quality of UK journalism, instrumental in making the UK government strive for reform, might have made Team Cameron overestimate the chances of winning reform allies among other member states. "Of course they will yield, the reform arguments are so strong!" However, a need for fundamental reform of the EU institutions is not even close to how things have typically been perceived among leading Swedish opinion makers.[68]

After the British government promised an EU referendum, and thereby upset the status quo way beyond the accepted limits in Sweden, the British Prime Minister was bound to be branded as the bad guy of Europe. In fact, he was a suspect already beforehand. Did he perhaps not lead the same party as (toxic brand) Margaret Thatcher? Had not the UK always been suspiciously pro (toxic brand) capitalism (forget the Conservative Party repositioning and forget the recent 13 years of Labour rule)? Was not the British Prime Minister, probably instigated by the 'rabid' right-wing press, on a crusade to try to force the unaware British voters towards a Brexit?

After years and years of voter conditioning along these lines politicians are actually holding themselves to ransom. Co-operating with a *conservative British government* (bad thing) in order to *remove powers from* the EU (favoured cause), would led to a double perception problem.

Since Team Cameron could not even win over a country such as Sweden the fight for real reform was more or less lost already beforehand. Yes, behind closed doors Swedish officials are always ready to assure any negotiator that they are certainly open to constructive arguments ('after all, the climate of debate in Sweden is superior, is it not?'). They will also let it be known that they, at least in part, understand every position ('there might actually be a few common concerns about the EU'). However, such declarations *never* transform into policies that fundamentally challenge the wisdom of internationalism. Politicians are well aware that after having uncritically peddled the internationalist gospel for decades they would, if now transgressing, immediately be hounded by the press corps they have taught to act as its champion.

A main reason EU scepticism among opinion makers is greater in the UK than in other member states is a higher quality journalism than on offer in probably any other EU member state country. The latter can be deduced from the fact that the debate over the EU, a controversial issue of crucial importance for the future, is much more vital in the UK than elsewhere. However, this is not so much because of much less biased individual reporting. There is no such thing as unbiased reporting; every media outlet (also in the UK) is biased in some way. British journalism instead draws its strength from the existence of a greater *range* of clashing positions disseminated from equally strong media platforms.

The lack of it, in far too many EU countries, is a major EU federalist asset. However, in conformist climates of debate swings can be sudden. If those frustrated by it reaches a critical mass the old song can turn out of fashion quite suddenly. 'Everyone' will then start competing to get on the new bandwagon and conveniently 'forget' old positions. When this happens the audience will once again have changed the direction of journalism and not the other way around.

*

2.11 Bias relating to moral prestige

Another bias, blatant to some but totally unseen by others, relates to the human striving to do something 'meaningful'. For many internationalists it has always been only moderately attractive to 'merely' administer something as technocratic and commercial as a free trade union or common market.

Strongly related to this attitude is the fact that 'lifestyle internationalists' often jump directly from a more or less politicised education, for example political science heavily coloured by a progressive thought model, into the, by its very nature, politicised public sphere. This means that a large number of internationalists never get near realities on the ground: the footwork at company level – both on the employer and employee side – which has always been required to raise productivity and ensure jobs. Too often is it possible to discern not only a lack of knowledge and understanding of the private sphere but also a somewhat arrogantly disrespectful attitude, including an arrogantly disrespectful attitude to the 'ordinary people' who every day deal with the economic challenges that *really* keep the wheels of society in motion. Closely related to this dilemma is the typical EU federalist self-image that human self-interest is much less at play within the EU than within other parts of society.

Arguably this attitude has played a key role when the EU, at astonishing speed, has been transformed from the single-minded free trade union or common market it was meant to be into an organisation which goes into areas that typically *have* a lot higher status in progressive circles than economy issues: peace issues, development aid, labour market policies, environmental issues, human rights.

The Lisbon treaty famously includes, just so, a special statute on human rights, the Charter of Fundamental Rights. Such statutes have always been a desideratum of politicians with expansionist ambitions. Who would not protect human rights? For politicians, this can then be used as an alibi to steer operations in almost any direction. Is it really compatible with human rights to permit abortion? To prohibit abortion? To not allow a flexible labour market, as this often implies less job security? To allow a flexible labour market, as this can be said to encourage the 'creative destruction' which leads to growth and job creation? Should homework be allowed even though this exposes children to achievement pressure? Should no homework be allowed despite the fact that education is crucial for both class mobility and for building individual self-esteem? Is it compatible with human rights to deport suspected villains to countries in which they are being sued by the victims of crime, even if prison conditions are poor? Or not? Is it compatible with human rights to allow, for instance, Christian Democratic parties which promote one religion over others? Or is it not compatible with human rights to disallow the Christian religion a special standing even though it is the by far the most supported religion within the EU? Is it compatible with human rights to allow all parties? Right-wing extremists? Communists? What about EU-sceptical parties? What about Jörg Haider's party in Austria? The EU sanctions failed that time, could and should something be done about that?

Indeed, within the EU sphere the perception is strong that the manifestly progressive side of the European project, the 'EU+' if you will, turns it into a force for moral good. The common market is sometimes regarded as not much more than a sort of necessary evil. Why is this bias so obvious to some but not even acknowledged by others? Simply because the internationalist narrative underpinning the European project is now so widespread and unquestioned by many – and alternative thought models so supressed - that it partly bears the hallmarks of a faith rather than what it really is: yet another convenient moral alibi for political centralisation.

It is presumably no coincidence that the last time a European organisation was developed with intimate political links to all European governments, it was an organisation which exercised monopoly rights as regards to human rights: the mediaeval Christian church.

*

2.12 Among 28 member states only the UK offers EU counterweight

The web of interests portrayed in this chapter go a long way in explaining why the EU, over the last decades, has been *constantly* expanding without more than minor objections from traditional opinion makers. With numerous spokespersons in all establishment parties and at all political levels in 28 countries, and with such vast resources to draw from, it is safe to say that the leading EU officials have, until very recently, quite fully controlled the official debate about itself. The absence of independent assessors certainly does not help. All national and supranational bodies that are supposed to professionally review the performance of the EU are themselves all deeply intertwined with the EU machinery. The result? The EU is in effect marking itself.

Such a situation is by no means unique in the history of politics. This chapter actually goes a long way in principally explaining how *all* political systems *always* have been crafted to support the dominant interest group(s) in society – unless clear and firm power checking mechanisms have been in place.

This is the main reason political systems that manage to gain the upper hand continue to grow. It explains why EU budget increases have become close to a normality, even when the member states are in deep economic trouble and need to make cuts in *national* budgets. Between 2007 and 2013, one of the worst crisis periods in modern times, the EU budget grew by around 30 percent.

In 2014, for the first time in the history of the EU, EU politicians were forced by its member states (spearheaded by the UK) to decrease expenses. However, after much resistance from Brussels the 2014 budget still turned out to be the second largest ever. The share of the administration costs continued to increase. Money was supposedly 'saved' elsewhere. Intriguingly, a practice of retroactive top-ups has also developed. This means that billions of euros might later be added to the approved budget.

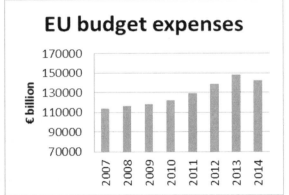

Source: EU Budget Financial Report 2014, European Commission

As regards to the vast arsenal of EU rules and regulations there is not a single dent in the growth curve. Also the number of people engaged within the vast EU umbrella has been continuously rising. Minor 'technical' points? Not at all. The more or less constant increase of such things reflects that all the dust kicked up by the 'major reform initiatives' pushed through by the EU officials, also during times of crisis, have always been synonymous with an also constant transferral of both money and political powers from the (net contributor) nation states to the EU.

Originally the EU *began* in a satellite position to Europe's national parliaments. In large parts it has now assumed control over its creators.

*

Then again, this is not only the doing of the EU federalists and their many apologists. Yes, there is indeed much to be said about bias and lack of sincere analysis and nuance but also voters are part of the story. It has always been difficult to win an election if not offering promises of hope. This is the case *even* if there is a utopian touch to such hopes. The pre-democratic right wing societies, built on the argument that some people are natural rulers while more divine than others, offered the hope of a perfect universal existence in the afterlife. Such a belief system would certainly not have been possible unless lots of people had bought into the narrative and then played the part. The pure socialistic societies, built on an academic construct including the notion that the road to freedom and prosperity was to disown ownership and 'temporary' freedom, offered the hope of a perfect future worldly existence. Also those societies, including the oppressive command and control system, would have been impossible without a large number of quite uncritical 'believers'. The EU, another academic construct that claims to benefit the people whether the people understands it or not, can correspondingly be perceived as the internationalist dream of a perfect society. Not only politicians but also many voters, not least well-educated urban middle class professionals, have pressed hard for the fulfilment of the internationalist promises. Sure, many voters have been led to swallow those promises but they would never have been entrenched had not many voters, collectively, demanded them.

Then again, it is certainly not easy but still easier to throw stones from the outside than from within. It is worth repeating that the forces at work shaping internal opinions are so strong that an individual, arguably, does not stand a chance against 'the system'. Then again, even if it would be close to inhuman to expect people working within to remain unaffected, this does not prevent the ill-effects. Quite the contrary, while strengthening the resolve of the system operators. Therefore stones *need* to be thrown from outside.

There is now good reason to doubt many of the EU promises: Fiscal responsibility. A currency union which lowers transaction costs while also bringing monetary stability to its member countries. Low unemployment. Social responsibility. Political stability. Security. Everyone working together in the same integrationist direction with no need to give alternative views any thought. No abuse of the tremendous powers given. Accomplished all at once by centralising the decision making *of no less than 28 countries* to administrators overseeing things from Brussels.

Who would not want all this? But what are the actual chances these promises will ever be fulfilled? The answer: Nil. A lot more about that in the next chapter.

Chapter 3: The six main reasons the EU will never fulfil its promises

With an understanding of the vested interests dominating the movers and shakers of the EU it is much easier to distinguish between PR-arguments and quality arguments. Thereafter it is, arguably, remarkably easy to conclude that the EU will never again be a well-functioning organisation. The reasons are summarised in this chapter.

*

3.1 The present set of EU promises are utopian

A useful rule of thumb is to ring the alarm bells as soon as politicians present universal solutions to millennium-old society problems. This irrespective of how seductively these universal solutions are presented. In fact, a second set of alarm bells should be ringing if the universal solutions are defended with lofty emotional arguments. Peace and prosperity are the two ultimate goals of just about everyone but no easy fix is available. If economic prosperity was ensured through centralisation then centralisation would have been realised long ago. If centralisation had also been the incomparably best peace guarantee, then the centralisation recipe would have been applied even earlier.

There is no perfect size of a state and never has been. If it is too small, then it risks being swallowed up or at least dominated by a larger neighbour. The gap between the decision- makers and the people will probably be smaller than in large populations but the climate of debate will be marked by conformity. One reason for the latter is that when the population is small, media outlets representing minority political opinion will always be hard to sustain economically. Moreover, in small countries most influential opinion makers tend to live and work within a few square kilometres in the capital. If being at odds with official wisdom it can lead not only to severe professional consequences, but also social.

If the state is too big, the number of bureaucratic layers will grow and so will the gap between the decision-makers and the people. The risk is considerable that it will lead to a poor understanding of both the realities on the ground and the public sentiment. After a while experience and understanding outside the public sphere might not even be considered valuable, only something that has to be pretended to be of value. The administrators will however readily liaise with academics who – in return for university funding - will offer 'expert' theoretic alibis for policies that increase the influence of politicians and bureaucrats. At some point these alibis will start to be regarded as truths. Politicians might very well start to argue that their interventions are *necessary* to preserve prosperity and peace. Moreover, taxpayer money will be used to create a gigantic PR (propaganda) machine which will override all others. Yet again the climate of debate will be marked by top down control rather than by a vigorous and thereby healthy debate.

One day the always increasing degree of intervention will start weakening rather than strengthening both the economy and the peace prospects. Slowly but steadily the public awareness of this development will be raised, which in turn will feed the flames of regional patriotism. It can be expected to happen first within countries economically strained which are also big net contributors to the EU budget. Another type of discontent can be expected in poorer countries which have grown used to generous funding that is no longer as forthcoming – simply because there is no longer as much money going around. At this point the centralisation project has not only overextended, it has started to *reinforce* regionalism and nationalism. However, the centralisers will, deliberately or not, mix up cause and effect and claim that it is the regionalism and nationalism that is dangerously destabilising.

The pattern just described has played out many times in history. During most parts of the last millennia the vast majority of societies have been micromanaged by a court which allegedly was authorised by God – and with the church providing a moral alibi. Just about every royal court sought to extend national borders. The degree of state intervention was massive, illustrated amongst others by Royal charters that swapped monopoly rights in exchange for royal commissions as well as total bans to carry on business outside the heavily regulated framework of the guilds. The considerable decision and tax privileges granted to the top administrators (aristocracy and clergy) reflected the perception that some people were not only worth more than others but also knew more than others. During this time the GNP grew at approximately 1 to 2% *per century*.[69] Wars were frequently fought, not least in order to divert attention from domestic discontent.

During the 20th century it was instead the helmsmen of socialism who 'in the name of the people' were particularly keen on micromanaging the economy. In all countries in which socialistic centralisation experiments were allowed free scope, for example the Soviet Union, the top administrators exerted even more state control than previous royals. They also lived considerably more privileged lives than normal citizens. There was no freedom of debate outside the Marxist doctrine but the top administrators were nevertheless (again) adamant that they possessed the skills and experiences needed to successfully command the economy. Up until the very end of the Soviet experiment world domination was deemed 'inevitable' and also a recipe for permanent friction with the rest of the world. Of course, the standard of living fell so drastically behind the standard of living in the Western world that the social system finally collapsed.

Today yet another attempt to create an omnipotent political system has been made: the EU. A novelty is that this system bears much more the marks of the middle-class than of either the aristocracy or the working class.

Once again a centrally governed political system has been established with people at the helm who, for alleged reasons of necessity, have proven perfectly willing to override democracy if needed to spread their tentacles of influence in all directions of society. This despite the strong *negative* link, over recent years, between economic performance and the level of economic integration; those countries that today synchronise their economies the most, the eurozone countries, have for quite a while made up the economically worst performing countries not only within the EU but in most parts of the world; The debt levels and levels of youth unemployment in many Southern European countries have reached disastrous levels. No surprise then that relative economic power is shifting from Europe – despite its massive head start. The blame game is on and political tensions between different regions of Europe are brewing. These are tensions that would not even have existed had the euro economies not been so deeply connected.

"God" is of course gone from the moral alibi underpinning the system equation and so is the belief in "total equality". In vogue is an equally hypothetical belief system, internationalism, which puts the concept of border dissolution centre stage. Meaning yet again a belief system perfectly suited to the political needs and purposes of the centralisers. The greatest beneficial difference is that there is a much stronger democratic element attached to the EU than to both the royalist and communist societies. However, it is not strong enough, meaning that it is not *truly* democratic, only less bad.

It is worth repeating that there has never been anything wrong – and still is nothing wrong - with the *initial* core promises of the European project. The EU system grew while it certainly makes sense that consumers, regardless of borders, are able to buy from those producers who are best at maximising value for money. Rewarding producer excellence means keeping up competitiveness against the rest of the world. This is the best recipe to also grow jobs and tax returns and thereby also welfare state financing abilities.

It might also be worth recalling that also the feudal system and the socialist system were connected with valuable core promises. The feudal system was originally built around the concept of work-for-(war)- lord-protection. This was a valuable exchange during a time when aggression was always close at hand and no standing army existed to deter even small bands of aggressors. With time a standing army *was* built but the lords kept their privileges despite no longer offering as much – or perhaps even any - protection in return. The socialist system grew on the back of offering a counterweight to the today so obvious injustices inherent in the aristocratic system. However, it is now well known that in some countries the fight for 'total equality' turned into a fight for conformity and brainwashing that left death and oppression in its trails.

In all three cases – the feudal system, the socialist command and control system and the EU system - successive political leaders have reached far *beyond* the healthy core promises, and thereby severely abused the goodwill that has surrounded the latter. Sure, many have acted in good faith while having been seduced by the internal messages of glorious purpose. That has aggravated the problem.

*

3.2 Trying to force nationhood will always provoke a backlash

The EU leaders are quite correct when claiming that neither national frontiers nor national responsibilities need to be regarded as cast in stone.

National frontiers are sometimes the result of geographic conditions but sometimes also the result of wars and chance. However, neither should national frontiers be treated lightly. The majority of European nations have common borders, laws and cultural traditions dating back many hundreds of years. These have survived simply due to broad popular support. Frontiers, traditions and laws can be defended with ever so many fine words but without popular support such words are practically worthless. When borders, laws and traditions change – without turmoil - it is because popular preferences have changed. Therefore it is also true that a country can and should be built on law and tradition but, crucially, it will only work if these laws and traditions are widely accepted.

Consequently, changes to something as central as the national frontiers or the constitution should not be forced, only when a people majority is clearly *ready* for change. The EU project arguably proves that it is possible to force change of this kind, *temporarily*, by underhanded methods. However, in the long run any such attempt is doomed to fail while a backlash will follow. With regards to the EU, that backlash is already well on its way.

The 'EU visionaries' see it quite differently. They typically predict that the preferences and attitudes of the EU citizens will merge into something distinctly Pan-European and that Europeans in due course will abandon or at least loosen nationalistic attachments. If the citizens of Europe do not presently understand the value of this it is right to work towards this objective anyway since, it is thought, the ambition serves the people. And people *will* come to understand the value, if not before as soon as the 'Erasmus generation' is in charge.[70]

The federalists also typically appear to regard it as petty to get hung up on minor matters and then miss "the big picture". A bit of democratic deficit here and a touch of overregulation there, but what is the importance of that compared to the magnificent superstructure! Here we are supposedly talking about something totally new and superior. Or, to use the words of Jacques Delors: "An empireless empire"."

However, any attempt to force people to consider 'Europe' as more important to their identity than nationhood is doomed to fail. There are five reasons:

Firstly, to believe strongly in the European project the EU would have to be commonly perceived as fulfilling its promises. It is not. While having let politics trump economics for too long, the EU federalists now have a hard time even defending the claim that it fulfils the core promise of economic vitality. Also popular belief in the EU security logic, underpinned by the highly abstract internationalist mindset, has been seriously dented after facing up to realities on the ground in, amongst others, Ukraine.

Secondly, the EU system is now too powerful and set in its ways to seriously accept and process counterarguments - in any other way than by playing the game of pretension. This means that prestige projects, such as the eurozone project, will continue to be defended at length despite design flaws that trump even basic economic logic. A political system that loses its capacity to self-improve is, arguably, heading nowhere but towards long term economic decline.

Thirdly, to feel affinity to the EU machinery Europeans have to gain much more knowledge about the people working within. Most people can name but a handful of people connected to the EU commission and the EU parliament, at best. Usually one of them is Nigel Farage. It is an uphill battle to gain a good understanding of anyone but those from the same nation. For a Brit or a Dane it is simply too time consuming to get to 'know' the representatives from Italy, Romania and Portugal. Moreover, it is probably not worth the effort. Since the EU officials vehemently avoid transparency few can anyway make out who really are the shakers and movers. Certainly, the EU officials *have to* keep the citizens of Europe in the dark in order to hide the constant horse trading, paper shuffling, grinding of pseudo arguments, lobbying, the power of the PR-people, the internal wars between entities with duplicated responsibilities, the condescending attitude towards voters as well as the constant debate over which tactic to use to grow the EU even further. However, this means they simultaneously maintain the barriers that are barriers to greater familiarity and voter acceptance.

Fourth, to claim that the vision is naive is an understatement. Toy for a moment with the thought that people would start perceiving the EU as delivering on its promises AND regard the Brussels bigwigs as real representatives of the people (rather than the representatives of either *other* people or the EU power experiment) AND that the officials in charge somehow can resist the narrative and power trappings that lead to stale thinking. Even then the problem remains that politicians and bureaucrats will always have a hard time accumulating the knowledge, experience and overview needed to plan and regulate a society that encompasses 500 million people, 28 (previous) societies and cultures and almost as many language zones. In addition, all these countries have separate bureaucracies that would need to be merged. In fact, believing that it even *could* work is arguably quite silly. Especially since the EU federalists have proven that they are certainly not satisfied if not allowed to dip their fingers in every single jar of jam besides possibly the tiniest ones. Actually, a belief in ground breaking improvement through a grand masterplan is - and always has been – less a sign of vision than a sign of *a lack of* vision.

A fifth reason, intimately intertwined with the fourth, is that when grandiose political centralisation projects are forced, nationalists always appear who gain political ground by demanding decentralisation. Such nationalists will be instrumental in punctuating 'the grand plan'. These will feed off the EU federalists and especially so when the latter manage to advance their cause. Why? Because then the federalists will face the incumbent problem: in line with their growing power they will increasingly be seen as in charge and will be held responsible for all sorts of ills, including those that it might (still) not be responsible for. That means the EU federalists will face some of their own music (as they have *always* used that very tactic against the nation states). At this point the quality of debate will reach a low point. Scapegoat politics will meet scapegoat politics.

What, then, about the US experience? Sometimes the EU federalists like to loosely compare the US Federation with a European federation. Is not US federalism evidence that the grand plan actually can work? Not really. The American colonizers were stumbling on virgin territory. Moreover, after having severed ties with the British empire the colonists had no old power structures to break (not least due to racism, imported from all over Europe, no local and regional power claims were taken seriously; without managing to unite and without weapons the Indians never stood a chance). Consequently the colonists could think afresh. So they did, sort of, when adopting a constitution which was in vogue among 'enlightened' people after the Glorious revolution (and birth of parliamentarianism). Moreover, there was never any real discussion about which language to use as the colonists from England dominated.

There was not even a need to harmonise local, regional and national bureaucracies because, if such even existed, they were rudimentary. Perhaps most importantly, when independence was declared in 1776, the total population of the new country amounted to 2.5 million people. That is 0.5 percent of the people now living within the EU borders. The European preconditions bear very little resemblance. Indeed, the rapid population growth in Europe over the last decades could be used to argue that as society – including the so called demos - is changing quickly anyway, now is certainly not the right time to also unravel well established national borders.

This still does not mean that the 'the vision of Europe' *has* to be ruled out. It does however mean that it can only be realised if and when – if ever – it starts to enjoy popular legitimacy. What *should* be totally ruled out is the attempt to force the vision from above, the vision has so many flaws that is simply will not work. Before Maastricht the European project *did* enjoy democratic legitimacy. Why then, not stop there and let things settle for a while without any predetermined undertakings about the future?

If everything is working well, and *if* the people stand ready to take another step, then so be it. If not, if the vast majority of people are happy with the borders that it has taken thousands of years and uncountable wars to settle, then it is better not to rock the boat.

As mentioned before, antagonism and wars rarely start (if ever) when *not* trying to change borders. Instead they typically start when powerful political leaders are trying to impose *new* grander borders and place themselves on top of a new power pyramid. This is of course the agenda of the supranationals, not the nationalists.

*

3.3 Europe is no longer a political experiment bank

For centuries many European countries have glanced furtively at one another's political systems as well as on one another's economic policies. If the political corruption has been too grave or the economic direction too strongly based on wishful theoretical thinking, such countries have lagged hopelessly behind. Countries that have proven more successful have been able to show the way. For example, parliamentarianism, born in the UK, proved to be such a superior form of government that all countries that did not follow trailed behind. Same thing with industrialisation. The UK led the way again which mirrors the strong connection between the two. Later on the UK, Germany and the Scandinavian countries acted as pioneer nations in regards to the development of the welfare state. This too proved to stimulate economic growth, not least through improving political stability. All other European countries with a similar socio-economic structure soon followed suit. When in the 1970s it appeared that the welfare state and public sector had grown to such a size that it undermined its own economic foundation, the United Kingdom (and the USA) went in the vanguard to create a new economic order. Again, regardless of government political colour, all other European countries followed (given that they were free to do so).

In a broader sense the element of actual plagiarising should not be overestimated. Most countries have evolved similarly while the internal political pressures have been following similar socioeconomic shifts. This is why the democratic systems cannot simply be adopted in a poor, say African, country regardless of how much its leaders or voters are glancing at the democratic development in richer countries. However, if countries *have* developed similarly there is every reason to plagiarise success recipes. This is precisely what has happened, over centuries, in Europe

Economic rivalry between neighbouring nation states has arguably played nothing less than a key role in Europe's tremendous economic and political success story since the start of industrialisation. Compare the European situation, since then, with the millennia-long period of economic stagnation and despotism in vast states such as China and Russia. The latter two states, which have been sufficiently large to somewhat ignore the rest of the world, are both centrally governed, heavily bureaucratized, depressingly corrupt while having embraced only one political and economic narrative at the time. Some of the wars these countries have fought have been called civil wars rather than wars between nation states. Military tension has nevertheless been a more or less constant feature. Sure, the political and economic structure of Europe is still a far cry from Russia's and China's. However, since the EU was born two decades ago Europe has arguably become more rather than less similar: more power centralisation, new layers of bureaucracy, new major outlets for corruption and power abuse and the EU has certainly also made the climate of debate much more conformist. Yes, both the Chinese and Russian economies have been partly transformed and have been growing rapidly over the last couple of decades but this is pretty much the first time in *documented* memory. Both countries are also growing from a level bordering on poverty and only after having steered somewhat in the direction of less power centralisation. Needless to say, the remaining structural problems in both countries are immense.

After the EC developed into the EU, the element of *trial and error* between Europe's nations has indeed gradually been 'co-ordinated' and 'harmonised' away. Not only has this meant that the EU has contributed to landing everyone in a similar mess, even more importantly, it has made it impossible for member states to get out of said mess while no longer allowed to try out a fundamentally different policies. It is easy to argue that this is particularly unfortunate as everyone is still learning the ropes in the new and now decidedly middle-class society.

If Europe's nations had still been fully free to chart their own paths, and thereby continue to serve as an experiment bank, there is good reason to believe that at least a few of these would already have shown the way by trying out different macroeconomic terrain.

It is telling that those countries with a greater degree of freedom, those outside the Eurozone, are, on a relative scale, in better shape than the rest.

What then about now turning to the USA, a vast federalist nation and, during the last two centuries, the greatest economic success story of all? Again the USA does not compare well precisely while, when colonised, it was virgin territory with vast amounts of largely untapped natural resources. Almost regardless of political system the US economy was bound to grow.

Today there is of course no virgin territory left meaning that individual states can no longer settle money matters 'simply' by developing backyard resources. There is now more scope of manoeuvre for the 'European' type of politicians who instead promise money either through redistribution from the more to the less affluent states or through artificial growth boosting (fiscal or monetary intervention). Crucially, both these remedies have had to be administered from Washington. The result? More power centralisation, a record breaking debt level and plenty of voter discontent. The politics of Europe and the USA is indeed converging – just not in a good way.

*

3.4 The unholy alliance between politicians and big lobbyists kills competitiveness

Any political parliament is, to a higher or lower degree, marked by rent-seeking[71] not only through the open and honest channels but also through underhanded lobbying, policy collusion, quid pro quo agreements[72], manipulations, back-door hidden agendas and *also special favours* for groups and individuals with lots of money and/or connections to the political top. If thinking about it realistically rather than ideologically this is a dilemma that will never be possible to fully eradicate. One interest group can assume power from another interest group with entrenched powers but that means that the backdoor efforts to control power and money will just shift hands.

What can be done is to try to *minimise* the impact of such dealings. Believing that there will be less misconduct behind closed doors is a too gullible notion for any adult. Consequently, what must *not* be done, if really acknowledging this issue to be a concern, is to hand over tremendous amounts of power to a political centre far removed from voters. Doing so would, arguably with hundred percent certainty, offer nothing less than structural support to *more* underhanded lobbying, *more* policy collusion, *more* manipulations, *more* back-door dealings and *less* protection for unorganised groups and individuals with little or no money. If doing so anyway it is easy to argue that it is then more or less a given that at least one of the following will happen:

a) Large corporations (landowners in the agricultural society) use their money advantage and lobbying clout to exploit the lower degree of transparency surrounding the legislation process in order to impose their will to an even higher degree than they would have been able to at a more decentralised level. This is the likely scenario during times when right-wing politicians are dominating the supranational scene. Standard motives used when doing so will be to protect competitive flexibility and ownership rights. In order to also protect the supranational platform of superior influence the well-capitalised corporations will turn into staunch federalist defenders. However, trade unions will be disadvantaged and will therefore act as a decentralising force.

b) Trade unions use their money and lobbying clout to exploit the very same lack of legislation transparency in order to impose their will to a much higher degree than they would be able to at a more decentralised level. This is the likely scenario when left-wing politicians are dominating the supranational scene. Standard motives used when doing so will be to protect employers from employer abuse and workers' rights. In order to protect the supranational platform of superior influence the well-capitalised trade unions will turn into staunch federalist defenders. However, private sector corporations will be disadvantaged and will therefore act as a decentralising force.

c) Large corporations *and* large trade unions collide with federalist politicians in order to carve out a system where major interest groups collide – or allow each other favoured subjects respite - at the cost of possibly small and medium sized organisations as well as taxpayers and consumers (typically unorganised and thereby easier to deceive). This is the likely scenario when centre ground politicians are dominating the supranational scene. Standard motives presented when doing so will be tailor-made to the situation at hand and can include anything that advances the federalist agenda: sometimes references will be made to workers' rights, sometimes to ownership rights and sometimes – and particularly deceptively – to taxpayers and consumers. It will be a politically easy sell while presented as capitalism but not "capitalism unleashed", instead "capitalism reined in". Consequently it will look fantastic – on paper. With both large corporations and trade unions on board there will be no strong establishment platform to provide a counterweight.

The centre ground - hybrid - line chosen will, yet again, be combining some of the worst aspects of the regulated society with the worst aspects of the free market. How so? Because an administrative burden will be imposed that would make it possible for politicians to claim they are maintaining thumbs in the eyes of the 'capitalists'. In a way this will be true but these 'capitalists' will readily accept such a burden while it will be much harder to cope with for smaller competitors (while not large enough to both take part in the lobbying game and also enjoy administrative scale benefits). Consequently the system systematically benefits the large industry players at the cost of the smaller ones and thereby encourages oligopolistic tendencies and rigid industry structures.

Many of the shapers of this system, the public servants more than the lobbyists, will probably be acting in good faith while not understanding the effect on the market: "We certainly do not like the big beasts so we keep them close in order to restrain them." Technically nothing in this statement, certainly helpful to many career public servants, is wrong. Yet the effect on society is highly damaging, especially long term, since the small and medium sized competitors typically are the job creators of the future.

Also early on a few 'dissenters' will point out that the establishment is ganging up on them but these will stand little chance when 'reasonable' middle-of-the-road public servants make common cause with big money lobbyists – and the tens of thousands of establishment apologists incorporated in the network of vested interests - and accuse such dissenters of believing in the bogeyman. The small and medium sized firms will be thrown a bone now and then, thereby creating confusion and making them toe the line. They will still struggle to catch a break, more than necessary, due to the anti-competitive regulatory policy collusion. The big beasts risk turning operationally complacent while increasingly relying on the political stich-up to stay profitable.

Sooner or later poor growth, poor profit margins and high unemployment numbers is likely to follow. At that point the system has turned counterproductive also for the big beasts. At last even some of them might start raising doubts, if so starting with the most competitive ones. However, all those having grown dependent on a de facto semi rigged market will point in every other direction to identify problem causes: "Perhaps some more monetary stimulation can put things right?"

*

3.5 Another bedrock of European strength, acceptance of political dissent, is also eroding

The convergence of views *within* national parliaments has played a severely underestimated role in the EU expansion story. Before the repositioning of many political parties towards the middle ground the centre of political opposition was *within* parliament. The grandest and most ideologically driven (utopian) ambitions of the left were always punctuated by the right – and vice versa. Today the dominant parties, all typically fighting for the middle ground, are often trying to stand out more with an original marketing package than by an original content.

This explains why the 'opposition parties' are often less inclined to genuinely contradict ideas than to triangulate (steal) them. It also explains why the political debates over content are often colourless and lacklustre. It moreover helps to explain why political theories constructed by the centre, such as the internationalist thinking underpinning the EU federalist logic, is so widely and readily accepted by the so called establishment that there is little 'serious' debate about its general validity.

It is no coincidence that the era of massive EU expansion coincides, in most European parliaments, with an era of more ideological conformity than at any point since the introduction of democracy. This is nothing less than the prime reason national politicians are *not* fulfilling the role of effective safeguards against EU mission creep and EU abuse. For too long the majority of MPs in most EU countries have, simply, been cut from more or less the same cloth as the EU federalists. Take the group of hugely influential EU commissioners. These are appointed by the member state governments and there is no sound reason - only sound explanations - that these commissioners should always be expansion advocates rather than advocates of an EU that is more in line with the original - less political - version of the European project. It is nevertheless hard to recall any EU Commissioner, with the last EU commissioner appointed by the UK as somewhat of an exception, who has *not* quite loudly been singing the EU expansion song.

Also this helps to explain why the fight for EU reform has assumed the character of the establishment versus the people rather than the political right versus the political left.

What about the spectators *outside* parliament? Voters and the media? Can they stimulate the debate when politicians do not? In the political system it is *intended* for both the people (voters) and the media (journalists) to play a spectator and catcalling role equivalent to that of football spectators when a football referee performs badly. These two roles are, arguably, often performed reasonably well on the national level where influential politicians often are well known and the dealings of government are (somewhat) possible to follow. However, already on the national level there are many problems relating to lack of insight. Neither voters nor journalists have nearly as good a view into the political system as the football spectator when he or she watches a football match. Into the political matches played in Brussels the voter has scarcely any insight at all. As regards to journalists, for reasons previously discussed, these are often represented by correspondents strongly inclined to simply pass on the official EU (PR) perspectives; after having added a few mild criticisms for the sake of appearance.

The absence of powerful independent assessors has made it possible for the by far most powerful political referee in Europe, the EU, to take sides FOR a whole range of politically useful (lobby) groups that it was and is supposed to referee impartially. These teams include the big (lending) banks, overconsuming mortgage holders, overspending governments even when breaking the 'golden rules' (at least up until the threat towards the euro project turned acute), migrants moving from the less prosperous countries, German exporters, French farmers, project initiators in less affluent regions of Europe who present project plans favourable to the EU federalist agenda when requesting grants and subsidies, EU federalist friendly academics, EU federalist friendly civil servants, EU federalist friendly politicians, EU federalist friendly consultants and EU federalist friendly journalists. Simultaneously the EU has proven to work AGAINST the interests of prudent savers, native job seekers in low income sectors, and producers in what used to be low cost countries within the eurozone. Small and medium sized companies across Europe which trade modestly or not at all with other countries - have no or little money to spare for lobbying purposes - but still need to handle two sets of regulations, politically easy targets within the finance sector, food (and clothes) consumers everywhere as well as net budget contributors and taxpayers everywhere caring about balancing their own books, but are still expected to foot the lion's share of the continuously expanding EU bill. The EU has also proven to work against all institutions and all people, including *truly* impartial academics, who have dared to raise even mild critique of the EU federalist agenda.

In fact, the dealings of the EU institutions are now so politicised and biased that the EU has gone way beyond the role of a referee. For quite some time it has, de facto, pro-actively *played along any* interest group in society that has helped to advance the EU federalist expansion agenda.

It should come as no surprise that many of those now disadvantaged have already lost trust in the EU federalists, despite (and perhaps partly because of) the level of heavily partisan 'EU information' that is disseminated on a daily basis. It is nothing but a charade to pretend that the majority of people in all countries but the UK want or should want 'ever closer union'. Already without ever having been offered a full take on things many voters know or suspect that EU decision making is marked by questionable undertakings. In one sense it is an insult to both the supposedly open public debate and democracy that the EU federalists, despite widespread scepticism, are able to pretty much dominate the *official* narrative in 27 member state countries. It the same sense it is close to tragicomic that the government in the 28th member state, the UK, is considered fiercely "EU sceptic" within the European establishment. This despite having, arguably, only cautiously and peripherally touched upon the fundamental problems facing the EU.

It is easy to declare this a massive failure of all politicians and civil servants who over the last couple of decades have claimed to be concerned about positive EU reform. It is a failure of all so called formal safeguards hailed by EU federalists – also nationally - as effective mechanisms against overreach. It is a failure of all those 'constitutional experts' who have not protested fiercely when the EU federalists have changed the rule book so as to avoid further people's referendums - as soon as it turned obvious that the people were no longer on board. In addition it is a massive failure of a vast number of academics and EU correspondents who present themselves as EU experts but have yet failed to present any genuinely serious critique. In the greater sense it is definitely a failure also of open debate and of democracy itself.

Accommodation of political dissent has been a bedrock of Western civilisation, perhaps its most distinguishing mark since the breakthrough of parliamentarianism. In fact, since the end of the era of the divine monarchs the history of European politics has to no small degree been a history of extending political power to new socioeconomic groups. More often than not progress has been painfully slow but over time progress has nevertheless been made. Not only have voting rights been extended but transparency has gradually improved.

For the first time in centuries both these processes are now in reverse. Again, immensely important political decisions are taken by people who have *not* been directly elected by the people. Again, lots of influential decisions are made behind doors which are not only firmly closed but also far, far away from voters.

The EU federalists still claim that the increasingly strong voter reactions are dangerous and destabilising. However, it is precisely the other way around. Had the EU federalists reined in their ambitions – and simultaneously allowed an honest debate - the political landscape would not be shapeshifting in a potentially dangerous way. However, if they continue to treat the parties of discontent as parties without any merit it will continue to give the latter nourishment. Which means that many traditional European parties will end up in a position when they have to adopt a more EU sceptic stance or be forced to stand aside as real power contenders. In the UK this process is, famously, already well on its way. The same development can be expected, with or without the UK as an EU member going forward, also in other European countries. Meaning that the EU has already reached its peak of power.

*

3.6 EU now fails the basic litmus test

Is it strange then that most EU politicians, despite everything, seem quite decent? Can the friendly Brussels faces be the orchestrators of today's mess? And is it *really* relevant to compare the power players of today's 'sophisticated' era with those of yesterday's 'brutal' era? The answer is a resounding yes, because that is precisely how yesterday's leaders were most commonly perceived during their heyday. The powers that be have always liked to portray the representatives of *earlier* political bodies of opinion as almost openly devilish. Going back as far as to the days of Shakespeare, his masterly portrayal of a supposed demon king, Richard III, would naturally not have been allowed when King Richard was still the ruler. However, his successors (the Tudor monarchs) were able to boost their controversial claims to the throne by Shakespeare's character assassination.

This leads into the dramaturgic reasons why *earlier* power structures tend to be described as autocratic and brutal. How would otherwise 'good' be able to defeat 'evil'? In reality, the distinction between good and evil has always, apart from during exceptional periods, been considerably more diffuse. *In all ages* the prominent power figures have tended to show the people good-natured smiles or faces burdened with responsibility. Indeed, these faces *have* been burdened. It is tiresome to hold power. Not only is there a constant need to deal with the 'normal' political agenda, but most of it is driven by events outside the control of any individual. On top of that there is the constant need to be on guard to avoid slipping up in the power game.

Yesterday's leaders were presumably just as convinced of their personal merits as today's leaders. Particularly in private conversation, the equally overwhelming majority of politicians and civil servants have always appeared to be decent people. In such contexts it has often been possible to gain a hearing for criticisms: 'Of course, I agree with a lot of your thoughts. Between four eyes I can tell you that also other people in the government as well as in parliament think precisely like you. Believe it or not but reforms are actually under way. At the same time, this is a sensitive issue. We have to bide our time. Just be patient, soon!'

Rumours that reforms are on the way have been used for centuries, quite effectively, in order to instil such an amount of hope that the disaffected will at least toe the line.

Simultaneously reforms of small importance have been dressed up as of great significance despite perhaps accomplishing nothing or close to nothing to solve the big structural problems. Often quite the opposite while stealing attention from what really matters.

This certainly does not mean that politicians and civil servants in general *are* to be regarded as indecent. It does however mean, as touched upon before, that the EU system is too powerful and self-preserving for any really free-thinking individual to stand a chance. A litmus test in any political system – and in any other organisation for that matter - is whether healthy constructive criticism is *seriously* welcomed. Does a politician or civil servant within the EU system have the opportunity to gain a hearing if he or she identifies and presents good reasons for restoring power to the member states? Or is that more likely to be synonymous with a dismissive pat on the head and a quiet career death? Is it a much better career move to act as the thought police for the EU apparatus and dismiss all advocates of downsizing as either 'racists', 'EU haters' or as 'people who think that all evil emanates from Brussels'? The painful truth is not particularly difficult to establish. Neither is it particularly surprising. Today's EU system arguably *invites* its employees and other dependents to embrace rather than resist the less flattering sides of human nature. For years many grown-ups have, arguably, been forced to present ingratiating, simplistic nonsense to prevent being chewed up and spat out of the EU apparatus. Such a situation is of course deeply undignified. It also renders the task at hand impossible: to safeguard the interests of the EU member states.

"The year was one of great political change in the EU. We have a new European Parliament, a new Commission and a new President of the European Council. This institutional renewal offers the opportunity of a new start for the EU. This time it has been different and we will do many different things and do them differently: 'big on the big things, small on the small things'."

(Jean-Claude Juncker summing up 2014)[73]

Today the Brussels institutions have the same sort of appeal as the royal palaces of the past. You do not really know what goes on within but the facades are bright and glittering. Authoritarian respect is expected and far too often granted. If you play along most people remain nice and polite and that is also the only way if aiming for a court career. However, if you start asking 'disloyal' questions smiles turn steely. Not only professional but also social ostracism is immediate. Now as before, those who believe that the decisions taken behind shiny palace gates serve society better than the decisions taken in the national parliament snake pits are gravely mistaken.

The historic equivalents of today's EU apologists are the Soviet Union apologists a few decades back and the aristocratic system apologists a few centuries back.

Chapter 4: Why staying within the EU is a recipe for a hazardous political stalemate

So, the EU has clearly overreached but there still appears to be public support for a common market. After all, a common market is precisely what was legitimised by voters during the referendum negotiations. Some like to say if this is the case then stop grumbling, roll up your sleeves, and push even harder for downscaling reform.

*

4.1 Big power houses such as the EU crumble before they change course

That argument might seem more appealing now while EU scepticism is more widespread. At least in theory this suggests that it is easier to gain a hearing.[74] However, realists will know that the playing field is rigged to a degree that makes major reform impossible.

There is overwhelming historical evidence that the political camp with the greatest economic muscle always wins 'the debate' simply while the largest money pot is synonymous with the largest number of spokespersons as well as the most frequently appearing messages. Over money no other camp is even close to competing with the EU federalists.

Taxpayers in 28 countries contribute to the EU ocean of PR-officials, many with euphemistic titles such as information officers or communicators. These PR-officials make sure that the official narrative is disseminated through the EU press releases, the EU information campaigns, the wealth of EU websites and publications, the thousands of daily contributions in social media, the heavily controlled Wikipedia entries relating to the EU and also news article comment fields. Search engine optimisation is also included in the list of duties which means that when members of the public try to seek out EU information over the Internet, results will be heavily skewed towards websites which are promoting the official narrative.

At the centre of these activities is an entire Directorate-General just for communications which is explicitly responsible for presenting the EU messages in a suitable way. In all member states there is also an EU

Commission 'representation office' as well as a European parliament 'information office'. Both of these can largely be regarded as de facto PR offices. In addition, the EU has established a network of local 'information centres' and 'documentation centres', on average about 20 per member state and around 50 in the UK.[75] Many of these branch out into the university sphere. There is also close cooperation between the EU administrators and EU-financed think tanks, newspapers, publishers and academic faculties.

Not even school children are left alone. Within the framework of a programme labelled 'EU-back to school' all EU politicians and officials could, ahead of the EU parliamentary election in 2014, draw on EU money and EU information material to visit schools and universities in their homeland. See text box for an example of the political 'balance' of this material which is still distributed to schools for free.

Two text samples in "Let's explore Europe!", a book which the European Commission Directorate-General for Communication recommends teachers to use against children aged 9-12.[76]

About the Common Agricultural Policy (p 31)

The Second World War had made it very difficult for Europe to produce food or to import it from other continents. Europe was short of food even in the early 1950s. So the EEC decided on an arrangement for paying its farmers to produce more food, and to make sure that they could earn a decent living from the land.

This arrangement was called the 'common agricultural policy' (or CAP). It worked well. So well, in fact, that farmers ended up producing too much food and the arrangement had to be changed! Nowadays, the CAP also pays farmers to look after the countryside.

About Peace (p 36)

The European Union has brought many European countries together in friendship. Of course, they don't always agree on everything but, instead of fighting, their leaders sit round a table to sort out their disagreements. So the dream of Jean Monnet and Robert Schuman has come true.

The EU has brought peace among its members.

No mention of any counterarguments or nuances. For example that Germany had to accept the hugely controversial (French) farming subsidies in order to be welcomed back into the international community. Or that Nato as well as the mutual Soviet threat facing Western Europe during the Cold War helped to maintain peace. No mention even of the fact that opposing views do exist. Such presentation of historic facts to school children certainly comes close to the definition of brainwashing: "To make someone believe something by repeatedly telling them that it is true and preventing any other information from reaching them".[77] Plenty of material produced in the same vein is offered also to university students.[78] This is a perfect example of how a dominating political camp writes - and disseminates - its own history.

Presumably there are not many organisations in the world as influential, wide reaching and well capitalised. The perhaps only challengers to the top title would be the Chinese Communist Party and the Russian propaganda apparatus. The US federalist PR machinery qualify in terms of reach and money but is not even close to the same level of influence while the US states, in contrast to the EU member states, offer staunch resistance to just about every centralisation attempt.

Ultimately it is PR-advantages that in all ages has made it possible to link utter gibberish to a healthy core idea - and then twist and repeat that gibberish until it has been widely believed. That is why so many member state governments across Europe still have not really challenged the present day gibberish that *friends* of Europe need to support the CAP, the eurozone project, geographic extension that violates 'golden rules' and a European Central Bank that for years has reinterpreted its treaty mandate to allow ever more lending to already heavily indebted borrowers. That is also why many are claiming that friends of Europe need to support a de facto EU Foreign Affairs ministry that is so deeply ingrained with a politically convenient academic construct - the internationalist thought model – that common sense holds little sway against it. And that friends of Europe need to maintain that Europe can cope with open borders and migration levels which bring all sorts of practical, economic and security problems - and thereby also a deeply destabilising political backlash.

The obvious trouble is that as long as (propaganda) money keeps pouring in deeply ingrained gibberish will continue to be promoted. Counterarguments will be drowned out or twisted in the flood of officially sanctioned 'information'. Problems incited or made worse by misguided centralisation policies will be presented as 'evidence' that even more centralisation is needed. Convenient scapegoats will be used to point fingers in every direction but in the direction of the EU policy architects.

The PR-power of Brussels, and the pointlessness of trying to accomplish EU reform that makes a real difference, was arguably well illustrated by the UK reform negotiations conducted during 2015 and 2016.

From a democratic perspective the calls for a referendum, first presented in 2013[79], are hardly unreasonable. What are referendums for if not to seek democratic legitimacy when a political decision is of both major importance and highly controversial? It is also noteworthy that the British referendum was proposed by a party leader, David Cameron, who from start openly declared that he wants to stay within the EU - given a renegotiated stance on issues of particular concern to the people. Still, already from the outset the EU integrationists talked about the reform demands as outrageous and the referendum as highly improper. This despite reform demands arguably distinguished by great modesty while not even close to what would really be needed to put things right.

Probably fully in line with intentions the Brussels federalists quickly managed to give the UK - and the Conservative party in particular - close to pariah status in official EU circles. In the end *no* major reform was accomplished with an EU wide impact. However, the UK relation was slightly recalibrated[80][81][82]. This can be regarded as an accomplishment of sorts given that not even one other member state government proved willing to offer the UK substantial support against the EU federalists.

The *most* remarkable thing, however, is that the EU federalists managed to isolate and arguably almost completely outplay one of its biggest member states, the UK, despite the latter making demands quite well in sync with what many European voters actually want. Managing to do this during a so called democratic era - and during a period marked by both the euro crisis and the immigration crisis - reflects the massive political clout of the EU federalists. It also reflects how their powers of interpretation ensure that the governments in no less than 27 out of 28 member states quite obediently toe the line even when the political ground is shaking. It moreover reflects how easy it still is, given institutional advantages and lots of money, to make nonsense of the public debate and thereby also of democracy.

*

4.2 Staying is likely to lead to a perpetual state of limbo that yet further weakens Europe

No organisation strong enough to push – and believe – nonsense can stay healthy. Consequently the end to the EU is easy to predict. Long term it stands no chance of surviving as anything but a memory of yet another paternalist megaproject that did not fulfil its splendid promises. However, history also proves that such systems, most of all due to their immensely powerful network, have a tendency to limp through, right until they fall and everyone starts saying they saw it coming. Muddle is the mark of any period of power balance and transition. Those wishing real change (voters) need to persuade still more undecideds before those resisting change (the establishment) can be forced to give in. The task for a politician is not envious during such circumstances. Almost every public servant wall will be shouting that it is 'unreasonable' and 'obstinate' to stir things up more than absolutely necessary – and thereby also destroy the legacy of most political patrons. At the same time increasingly vocal voters will be shouting "Don't you get it?" Only in such a conflicting opinion climate is it possible with a referendum about sort-of-reform and politicians who stake their careers on a sort-of-result.

Due to the reasons mentioned in chapter two there is no danger at all that the EU federalists eventually manage to fulfil its vainglorious and perilous ambition to create one European Super-state. There is however a real danger of a long-lasting political stalemate between those advocating downscaling and those advocating integration. The former will be empowered by disillusioned voters and the latter by their institutional advantages. While both sides might be sufficiently powerful to block each other there is indeed a great risk that Europe will remain in its present state of mutual dissatisfaction and quintuple limbo situation: no convincing economic narrative, no convincing security narrative, no convincing migration narrative, greater distrust of politicians than at any previous point since the introduction of democracy and no chance of a fundamental rethink at the top of the power pyramid. Add to this that the EU debate in the UK is a model of excellence compared to the EU debate among possibly all other 27 member states - despite the major institutional advantages of the EU apologists also in the UK. This means that the so called serious European debate outside the UK is not particularly serious at all. It still rather bears the mark of the same conformity and politically useful virtue signalling that distinguish all narratives heavily guided by vested interests. Moreover, the element of democracy that still does exist makes it impossible for the EU federalists to turn *totally* idealistic in their everyday activities. If some group in some country starts crying loud enough they will be thrown just enough of a bone to diffuse the protest movement – or at least diffuse it enough not to have to abandon the general course. This makes it possible to just about scrape by.

Indeed, if someone deliberately had tried to cook up a recipe for making European affairs go sideways it is hard to see how the present condition could have been bettered.

With the political stars aligned to scrape by, it is easy to argue that the *best case* scenario, if staying within the EU, is a couple of economically lost 'Japanese' decades. The worst case scenario involves *lower* living standards, disastrously high levels of youth unemployment in Southern Europe (also going forward), possibly civil unrest, a perpetual blame game and - eventually - 'strong men' yet again arising across Europe 'to put things right'. In both scenarios the eventual EU implosion is inevitable.

Chapter 5: But the now inevitable EU downfall will be an opportunity to start afresh

Among the EU federalists it is of course heresy to even think of leaving the EU. Both directly and indirectly people like Barroso and Juncker have claimed, on numerous occasions, that peace and prosperity would be threatened and our world change forever. That is precisely the way the royals and their dependents spoke 150 years ago. It is also the way the Soviet leaders and their minions spoke only a few decades ago.

Those political leaders who had invested heavily in the systems cracking – and the paternalist romanticism underpinning them - bought additional time simply by presenting mirror image scare stories, often concluding with the warning that drastic measures should *not* be taken during turbulent times. Crucially however, when counterweight was at last imposed, it *led to* greater amounts of stability and prosperity, not the reverse.

If leaving the EU the common market can certainly be recreated. Moreover, whenever it happens, it most likely will.

*

5.1 Brexit would improve both growth and peace prospects

Following Brexit lots of huffing and puffing would no doubt follow but after a fait accompli the chessboard would be completely overturned. This would mean an equally revised incentive structure which arguably would work to the advantage of the UK.

5.1.1 Trading would carry on regardless of the political show(s)

European politicians today threatening to punish the UK for its 'transgression' would have a hard time doing so in practice. Why?

Firstly, the EU federalists will find themselves held in check – or replaced - by an increasingly EU critical electorate also in other EU member states.

Secondly, profits and jobs in many European corporations are partly dependent on UK sales. Many such corporations - and involved trade unions - are influential party sponsors all across Europe and they will also hold the punishers in check. In fact, the unholy alliance between the

EU federalists and big money is what holds the EU together. If also the big corporations and trade unions finally start complaining the EU federalist game would be up all across Europe – and within months rather than years.

Thirdly, many EU public servants today specialising on the UK relationship will work hard to create new spaces for themselves. They will want to minimise their loss by establishing a new long-standing arrangement and – from their personal perspective – the bigger the better.

Fourth, the fact that the UK is the third largest net contributor to the EU budget would be a great bargaining chip. EU federalists having grown used to yearly budget increases will be desperate to minimise the loss of money presently taken for granted. They will undoubtedly try to keep some of that money as a 'market access fee'. However, that means that market access also has to be given.

Fifth, while trapped in a sclerotic union and dependent on jobs and taxes generated in the private sector the EU core countries *need* trading partners – even in 'treacherous' countries having left. They will especially need British trading partners since the UK, by then, will have transformed into the by far largest economy neighbouring the EU.

Sixth, disentangling of trading arrangements from the political overcoat will lead to less vagueness as to the value of market access. Meaning that the EU federalists will no longer be able to dilute the UK trading position by claiming that so much more is gained than 'just' access to the common market. In this respect the UK negotiating position would, arguably, be strengthened.

Seventh, downward pressure on tariffs is exerted also via the World Trade Organisation and the EU would, in all events, not be able to deviate too much from the norm between developed states.

Eight, the EU federalists would find themselves caught in their own narrative. If maintaining that their form of association really is superior - the common market plus the massive political overcoat today making up the EU - they should have nothing to fear by concluding something more similar to only a common market agreement. What, after all, would they tell their own voters if refusing to do so? "British voters have decided to leave our club. Now they need to be punished! This means that you need to accept that from now on neither can sell them your products nor buy theirs." Moreover, if it really is a project meant to serve its members rather than a power project, is it not quite natural if a member not convinced of its merits beyond trading is offered, just so, a trading relationship, thereby simultaneously making it easier for remaining members to push forward in a direction in line with their beliefs.

Sure, in order to access the common market other European nations having remained outside the EU, today notably Norway and Switzerland, have to obediently conform to EU market standards. However, inside or outside, small countries such as Norway and Switzerland have very little say either way. Living in the shadows of a large political entity means, in practice, little say in trading matters regardless of how much public servants in small member states *claim* influence when facing *domestic* audiences. Outside the EU even the UK would have to quite obediently conform to EU *trading* standards. However, this would not differ much from how UK companies have to accept US market standards when trading with the USA and Chinese market standards when trading with China. In addition, when it comes to deciding the nuts and bolts of realising a common market it might not be crucial to have lots to say. The important thing is often to decide on *one* standard – not which one.

As an external trading partner the UK would, while the fifth largest economy in the world, have a much stronger bargaining position than Norway and Switzerland when negotiating new relationship terms. If it at all would have to pay for market access (as they do) the figure would certainly amount to much less than the around 14 billion euros which UK taxpayers today contribute to the EU budget (British EU stakeholders get back around half the taxpayer gross contribution). As a result plenty of taxpayer money would be freed up which, amongst others, could be used to compensate such British EU stakeholders.

Public servants have always liked to blow their own trumpets as regards to their importance when moulding trading relationships. In practice they have also always been more of middle-men than architects.

In a controversial EU leaflet distributed to UK households on April 11 2016 the government claims to set out the facts about the EU but still (amongst many other arguably dubious claims) associate low cost flights as well as diminishing phone roaming charges to the work of the EU.[83] This fundamentally misrepresents how change of that nature is realised. Low cost flights are, ironically, the result of local airport operators and local politicians competing for business, while flights bring tourists that can rejuvenate an entire region. Together these participants have created pressure within the political system to make it happen and since the EU has assumed the ultimate political control they have – as the *last* instance - be called to act accordingly. Similar story with mobile phone charges. If too expensive consumers simply do not telephone when abroad. Hence a profit incentive for mobile phone operators to make international deals with other phone operators while pressuring politicians to cut tariffs. Sure, the EU is involved but yet again the EU is not the process initiator and developments such as these would not be much different had the EU not existed. Perhaps it would even have been easier. UK politicians acting on behalf of the British phone operator industry would have concluded a deal with their French counterparts. The agreement would have been used as a template when concluding deals also with other countries. With or without the existence of the EU an international mobile operator trade association would have acted as a facilitator.[84]

If large corporations, large trade unions, consumers and local politicians all want trade then trade *will* happen. And almost always all such market participants do want trade besides sometimes corporations and trade unions linked to uncompetitive industries. The latter industries will, as always, push for protectionism.

However, also the EU federalists will be aware that if favouring the uncompetitive industries over the competitive ever more people will, for good reason, write off the EU project as interventionist, inward-looking and sclerotic.

5.1.2 Distinct improvements on many fronts

Leaving a large trading area while then having to negotiate your way back in order to trade is, admittedly, not intuitively appealing. However, there are drawbacks either way and the EU can be used almost as evidence that adding a powerful political overcoat to a common market area will go a long way in actually defeating the purpose of the latter. How so? Because if internationalist bureaucrats gain a position of strength a web of vested interests will probably always be spun that ensures continuous organisational growth. A never ending stream of interventions will be presented as 'absolutely necessary', not always because of their usefulness to society but while needed to motivate higher budgets and yet more people. This will bring lots of extra red tape. The plights of people in less vital regions will typically be used as a handy excuse for a centrally planned money redistribution circus that locks such regions into economic dependence. Many public servants will consider themselves not only above trading matters – as public servants often do – but also doubt the power of a common market to maximise growth, jobs and taxes. Some will be quite set on "reining in the capitalists" and be unaware or simply do not mind that the freedom aspect of the supposedly free market is then continuously eroded. The same public servants will often be happy to enter into arrangements with big money lobbyists who accept more regulations. All might not even understand that they will then, in practice, take part in rigging the prevailing industry structure in favour of the, yes, already big players. Certainly, many public servants driving centralisation will be acting in good faith but, as previously discussed, this will not help. Rather the opposite.

Going forward there will still be lots of *talk* about promoting the common market – that is after all why the organisation was created in the first place. Massive PR-budgets will help to hide that the free trade purpose is no longer a primary concern. By then the organisation will have partly transformed into a job magnet for internationalists rather than a trade facilitator.

When club members are being warned they cannot leave and that they should expect punishing circumstances if doing so anyway, then it is quite evident something is fundamentally amiss. Is it definitely still *a* market but is it still a free market? And why would anyone need to be forced to stay in a club supposedly created to serve the best interests of its members?

The offer of free trade and no or little meddling in member state matters is long gone from the EU table. Moreover, such are the EU federalist ambitions for the future that there is no chance that this offer will ever come back. The appeal of leaving is not only that it is unwise to stay attached to a sinking ship but also that it would provide an immediate opportunity to start afresh. True, no one can tell what will happen in any detail, if leaving, but four things directly related to trading are arguably certain:

First, for reasons recently explained a new trading relationship *will* be established. When the EU federalists are saying that the current relationships are excruciatingly complex and close to impossible to entangle scare tactics are adopted. Any legal text can quite easily be made void and rewritten as long as all parties involved agree (also, if a relationship really is excruciatingly complex this might be sufficient reason to seek simplification.)

Second, due to the mutual need to trade there will not be as much drama when shaping the new relationship as some people expect or pretend to expect. Instead of big bang moments a new relationship will probably be established in a piecemeal way[85]. Simply while less complicated trading arrangements relating to goods might be settled before trading arrangements relating to services[86]. Illustrated not least by the EU example: trading arrangements relating to services are still far from not settled which reduces the service industry impact of leaving.

Some old arrangements, in place before the EC received its political overcoat, might be dusted off and updated, which could mean a return to the 'default settings' before the relationship turned controversial. Issues not covered are likely to be solved on a tailor-made basis.

Thirdly, if staying there will be great amounts of uncertainty over trading relationship terms; not least while also staying will entail changed relationship terms. Changes which, as before, take place through mission creep. The EU system is simply geared in that way. No one can tell how much this will continue to dampen future growth prospects. Indeed, most reports attempting to calculate growth effects are more or less pointless while being too partial. Just about every observer claims 'independence' and yet it almost never happens that anyone, after 'careful scrutiny of the numbers', comes up with reports not helpful to the camp already favoured. Number crunchers who claim neutrality and refuse to commit either way – and thereby keep their options open - are no less politicised if *always* arriving at the then somewhat too convenient conclusion that the net effect will be 'small'.

Fourth, the full dynamic effects are rarely included in any economic calculation. One reason is that such effects are hard or impossible to quantify. However, the reason many of these effects are rarely even mentioned is that the EU federalists certainly do not want them mentioned. Much preferred to them is a single minded focus on tariffs while forcing EU critics on the defensive. However, even a few extra tariff points here and there on goods and services is arguably of minor significance compared to the costs of the following:

- Costs relating to money misspent or wasted in the EU money circus: member state fees going to Brussels administrators who, after having taken a 'commission', dish out parts of the money to EU friendly project initiators. Much of this money could most certainly be put to better use especially if locking entire regions into economic dependence while serving the Brussels centralisation agenda.
- Costs associated with placing the political power centre further from the scrutiny of the people thereby in effect promoting a system in which underhanded lobbying and all sorts of backroom dealings always turn into distinguishing marks.
- Costs relating to EU public servants not really needed who have a personal incentive to make up excuses to dabble around in order to motivate their own existence.
- Costs relating to member state public servants making flawed centralisation decisions when smelling international career opportunities.
- Costs relating to nations having a currency that is either undervalued (for example Germany) or overvalued (for example Greece).
- Costs associated with a political system in which it means career death if seriously challenging the most convenient official 'truths'.
- Costs, potentially limitless, connected with a peace paradigm based on wishful thinking.
- Costs, again potentially limitless, linked to the political friction generated because of the EU federalist attempt to yet again reshape the borders of Europe, despite many precedents with an explosive outcome.
- Costs relating to the political instability that has followed due to the counterproductive EU meddling in member state migration policies.
- Costs of opportunities lost when member states no longer have the freedom to individually conclude alternative trading arrangements – or change them if no longer considered useful.

- Costs of opportunities lost associated with the EU having made sure that Europe is much less of a political experiment bank than it used to be.
- Costs of opportunities lost associated with the corporatist regulatory arrangements between EU administrators and big money lobbyists – especially due to the dampening effects on entrepreneurial activities.
- Costs associated with the EU federalists having groomed generations of students into an uncritical – and thereby totally unscientific - view of the EU.
- Perhaps most crucially, there are astronomical costs associated with the dramatically reduced quality of the public political debate. By de facto having bought the support of tens of thousands so called pillars of society - including leading politicians, civil servants and academics across Europe – there is much less scope for dissent. As already touched upon, a broad scope for dissent used to be the bedrock of European strength.

If incorporating also these costs there can arguably be little doubt that Brexit would have a long term *positive* effect both politically and economically.

Sure, leaving the money circus in Brussels would partly be replaced by a money circus orchestrated from London. Money would still be wasted but, crucially, not nearly as much, while decisions would be taken closer to *real* scrutinisers (voters and journalists). Also, a couple of expensive layers of bureaucrats (those on the supranational level) would be removed (and those left nationally would be quite sufficient for administration purposes). Most importantly, the decision quality would improve while officials would no longer be under the spell of Brussels.

Summing up the economic consequences of a Brexit it arguably would be reasonable to expect a short term negative impact (mainly due to psychology and doomsayer prophecies still fresh in people's minds), little if any medium term impact (there will be a growing understanding that the sun will continue to rise but the positive dynamic effects are yet to be reaped) and a markedly positive long term impact.

5.1.3 Some things such as security will simply stay much the same

Many things that the EU federalists claim much credit for will prove to stay just about the same while based on a functional need over which EU membership has little effect. For example security co-operation would, regardless of EU federalist claims to the contrary, largely carry on as before. Due to American military strength Nato will continue to be the epicentre of military co-operation. The UK, the world's fourth most important military power, will continue to be part of every important discussion concerning the military security of Europe.

During dangerous situations the prime discussions will take place directly between Berlin, Paris, London and Washington, outside the EU scope. This is the case also today. Regarding intelligence, sharing old arrangements might be given new names but, again precisely as before, they will continue to be shared with other countries based on functional merit; important secret intelligence has never been shared with all 28 EU member countries. Many opinion makers have already pointed out that sharing intelligence across the EU would be a fool proof way of not letting it remain secret.

Leaving the EU would indeed bring three significant security advantages. Firstly, fewer people will have influence over security issues who *need* to, for career reasons, push the misguided internationalist peace agenda. This means that realism will stand a better chance against dangerous gullibility. Secondly, as mentioned before, economic growth is ultimately the guarantor of both domestic and international peace. Since the EU of today no longer is a great growth promoter, leaving and starting afresh would improve not only growth but also peace prospects.

Thirdly, friction *caused* by the EU will diminish at least if other member states follow the UK example and also leave the EU. There is indeed much existing suspicion and friction between member states that could have been avoided had not the EU demanded ever more 'togetherness'. Take the three dominant European powers: the UK, France and Germany. None of them are natural bedfellows. However, every pairing can and will talk shop when really necessary. *If* the relationship has not turned sour due to constant EU federalist conformity pressures – pressures that just keep coming despite deviating interests and preferences. The EU federalists consider even the suggestion blasphemous but relationships based on compulsion can sometimes be saved by *looser* ties.

5.1.4 And a trade facilitator that actually works could be re-established

After a Brexit the UK would be free to join forces with other nations believing in the value and attractiveness of a common market. An investigation into the possibilities of making common cause with the Efta countries would soon follow. If the UK was to start co-operating with Norway and Switzerland the Efta might not survive in its current shape due both to the size of the UK and the currently fragmented nature of the Efta country relationships with the EU. However, the UK, Switzerland and Norway might want to agree to form what could be dubbed 'EC II', a new facilitator of neither more, nor less, than international trade. Some other EU countries might follow at a surprising speed since a Brexit would immediately make the EU less competitive and attractive to many other EU member states, especially to other net budget contributors. Moreover, without a political overcoat the new trading facilitator could be genuinely outward looking and include likeminded nations also *outside* Europe, for example other commonwealth nations (which naturally would force a name change). Needless to say, a free trade agreement with the United States would be high up on the agenda. EC II might even beat the EU to it (negotiations over a comprehensive free trade agreement between the EU and the United States have carried on for years and still appear to be far from a conclusion). Not only would EC II be an easier negotiating partner while a lean organisation without hidden political agendas, it would also include a country (the UK) with deep rooted American businesses ties – including business ties existing long before the birth of the EU.

*

5.2 Avoid the EU design mistakes when recreating a common market

Whatever the shape of the trading arrangements of the future there are three major mistakes when the EU was designed which must never be repeated.

5.2.1 Establish clear limits to the mandate of any new trading facilitator

A first *rule of thumb* if and when establishing a new trading facilitator treaty, still named EC II for the purposes of this book, is to establish that the main purpose is to solely promote trade between member states;

nothing more and nothing less. Thereby producers in every country involved will be able to produce and sell what they are best at producing. The explicit purpose should be to promote growth, job creation and the tax base needed to amongst others fund the welfare state. This is precisely what most member states first signed up to when joining the EC or the EU. While this is also what still seems to be widely supported by the public it would ensure political stability.

A second rule of thumb, intimately related to the first, should be to depoliticise the EC II by leaving the politically toxic issues to either national parliaments or to *other* international organisations.

As mentioned previously, the idea of an international body that promotes international trade has never been particularly politically toxic besides amongst 'left-wing radicals' (presumably those who dispute that free trade benefits the working class) and 'right-wing radicals' (presumably those who suspect anything taking place outside national borders). Despite politically motivated efforts to talk up the political importance of these two groups, none are particularly influential. The real political fissures emerge when the mandate is widened *beyond* free trade since that is when political divisions are created also among 'moderates'.

As a consequence EC II must *not* involve itself in the following: foreign policy, migration policies, labour market policies, monetary policies, bank lending practices, agricultural policies, social cohesion policies, human rights and environmental issues (more about this in the next section).

A third rule of thumb should be to ensure a short treaty text. Today there is no person alive that could clearly define what powers have and have not been given to the EU. There are simply too much text – altogether thousands of pages of treaty text – including too much vague phraseology and too many full-on contradictions, including simultaneous adherence both to ever closer union and subsidiarity. This leaves, as possibly intended, a wide scope for subjective interpretation and mission creep. A new treaty could be written which is no longer than half the size of the American Constitution (the latter amounts to 8700 words). A short treaty would imply clear thinking. Making it half the size of the American Constitution would signal that the EC II is *not* a state and does not need all the treaty provisions of a state. This means that EC II should be an entity of so called limited powers; it should possess only such powers specifically granted to it in the treaty. It should strive for nothing more and nothing less.

Already several hundred years ago the 'fathers of power separation' - people like John Locke, Montesquieu and James Madison – understood the importance of clearly defining where political powers begin and end. These intellectual giants all concluded that if political constitutions and treaties do not both grant *and* restrict powers, arbitrary and creeping expansion of power – and worse, abuse – will follow.

5.2.2 *Separate other international arrangements*

A fourth rule of thumb should be, when international co-operation really *is* warranted, to separate policy areas in *different* international organisations. The EC II could be the natural point of gravity when it comes to realising a free trade area; the Council of Europe could deal with human rights; the World Trade Organisation could be responsible for global monopoly and oligopoly issues; the World Health Organisation could assume full control of international health issues; Interpol could assume control over international police issues (or Europol); NATO over security arrangements; UN over multilateral aid (UNDP), global environment issues (UNEP) and refugee issues (UNHCR) even if preferably first after having been reformed in line with a realist approach. International dealings relating to the labour market – including workplace health and safety issues - could, just as before the EU was born, take place within the framework of international employer and employee associations.

The EU federalist sometimes point out that leaving includes a risk of ending up with a world order reeking from 19th century nationalism and protectionism. However, going back only two decades comes closer to a much more likely scenario. Reshaping the international order of the early 1990s - not a bad time when it comes to international co-operation - could and probably would follow almost automatically. There are countries which do want to trade without attaching a political overcoat to the trading mechanisms. Consequently it will happen. The institutional framework for international co-operation beyond that is already in place. Many international organisations would probably, secretly, be welcoming if the EU stopped overlapping their activities. There is good reason to argue that the risk of going back to an era of dangerous nationalism and protectionism is much greater than staying since the EU itself is the by far most important current nourisher of both nationalism and the scepticism now surrounding international co-operation.

The EU federalists would most likely say that organisational separation increases the total administrative burden but the opposite would most certainly be true. Separation would mean avoidance of work duplication. It would also help to keep each and every organisation reasonably slim and manageable since bureaucratic dead wood would be easier to identify. Overall transparency would be improved. As every international organisation would assume full area responsibility, disentanglement would also make it possible to reap tremendous benefits relating to both attention focus and accountability. Nonetheless, the most important benefit of them all would be that clear and explicit power separation of international activities would hinder the EU from remaining the *Mädchen für alles* that it is today; an entity that has already partly succeeded in turning the nation states into dependents simply while sufficiently strong to make it happen.

5.2.3 Stop listening to career idealists

If a private corporation, say Coca Cola, would fund a professor or cultural institution to praise the virtues of Coca Cola nobody would take such professors or cultural institutions seriously. For decades the EU has nevertheless got away with the equivalent trick. It still does.

For years many university professors, and other 'EU experts', have systematically broadcasted the EU federalist narrative as if it is underpinned by undisputed facts.

A fifth rule of thumb should be to check the funding source(s) of those writing the 'independent assessment reports'. Is there a system of mutual backscratching between those craving a growth alibi and those providing such an alibi? Have experts consulted by the government ever ventured to offer opinions *not* well in sync with what is politically convenient? If not, pick someone else.

Chapter 6: Epilogue

The European project, when it focused exclusively on the common market, was certainly grand. Even grander would it have been if that focus had been maintained without catching political hubris. It is precisely because of such hubris it is no longer a question of if the EU will implode – but when.

*

It is the EU that has changed, not voters who have legitimised neither more nor less than a common market, meaning that the EU has betrayed its members, not the other way around.

*

The EU has actually been destined to fail almost from the outset. Handing huge amounts of power and money to administrators far removed from the watchful eyes of voters and media – while attaching no power limits – is a fool proof recipe for overshoot.

*

No political problem would exist without flaws in human nature. The best thing to do to mitigate rather than accentuate human flaws is to keep decision makers close. This also just happens to be the superior way to bring out the decent sides of human nature. Sending them off to a different country is synonymous with also inviting power abuse.

*

The EU represents a return to a time when the political system was underpinned by the romantic and highly paternalistic notion that all will be well if only trusting the words of the friendly people in power. Friendly paternalistic right-wingers had their chance before democracy and they blew it. Friendly paternalistic left-wingers had their chance in many countries during the 20th century. They also blew it. The EU can be taken as evidence that also friendly middle-of-the-road internationalists will, if given the chance, be paternalistic and power maximising. It takes the fervour of a zealot not to see they also have blown it.

*

Had it been possible to return to basics by changing from within that would have been the preferred choice. However, those thinking this possible have failed to understand the strength of the power mechanisms defending a deeply entrenched political narrative.

*

The EU federalisers, just as every power centralisers before them, have used their immense powers of interpretation to claim ownership to every emotionally positive term while sticking everything emotionally negative to their opponents. Now as always the moral alibi presented is perfectly adapted to the emotional triggers of the currently dominant socioeconomic group (the middle class); especially the notion of caring more than others for the poor and suffering is peddled with, as also always before, extra gusto. Still, power centralisation has never spelt good news for those really in need.

*

The academic sector is as useful as a political tool as in any previous era: professors and researchers specialising on the EU and willing to serve as A+ marksmen gain more funding, prestigious government assignments and media exposure. The political usefulness of the academic sector does not stop there. Also the trick of first grooming students into the 'right' political beliefs and then highlighting their views as the views of the 'generation of the future' is as old as the university sphere itself.

*

The EU integrationist fight to perfect society is fought by highlighting the warts in the current one. These type of fights, yet again with many dangerous echoes in history, have always appealed simply while warts have also always been easy to spot all over the place. Then again, political megaprojects *always* lead to grave disappointments – and more imperfection than at the outset.

*

Those claiming they can do better will either be opportunists or romantics (or both). They will also be putting everything gained at risk. There is certainly much to lose. What large parts of Europe has been privileged with since 1945 - in terms of democracy, freedom, tolerance, continuously raised high living standards and nation states co-existing without challenging each other's borders - is a lot easier to underestimate than overestimate. The EC played an important role in making this happen. The EU has not.

*

The fight to contain the EU federalists is nothing less than a fight to preserve a political model which, despite warts and all, beats all others tested.

*

No true democrat would persuade themselves that he or she really is a true democrat *despite* treating people's consultations as unnecessary irritations. It takes an armchair thinker who considers people empowerment as an abstract notion and a sort of 'nice' addition – if and only if the grandiose academic plans are accepted.

*

Still, people empowerment is nothing less than *the key* to what has made Europe so immensely fortunate, over the last centuries, compared to most other continents. The degree of people empowerment directly affects to what degree the creative potential of the people is tapped into. It is the ultimate guarantor of reality attachment, diversity of political ideas and quick readjustment when things go sideways. Consequently it is the ultimate underwriter of political health. It is moreover a guarantor of a counterbalance to stitch ups between politicians and big money. Consequently it is also an underwriter of a more level playing field for small scale entrepreneurs: the future job and tax generators.

*

It is commonly claimed that the first duty of government is to protect its citizens. Another top priority is to support economic growth in order to maintain and hopefully improve the already achieved living standards and employment levels. These are no doubt priorities of essential importance to society. A main conclusion from this book, however, is that the *very* first duty of government needs to be to make sure that democracy is never eroded. Only regular people's consultations can make sure not only that decisions are legitimised and thereby respected (guarantees stability) but also a public discourse in touch with realities on the ground (guarantees more qualified decision making). Allowing a significant amount of democratic deficit means entering a slippery slope while just as significantly boosting the prospects of paternalists; either of the 'strongman' kind that offers clear direction but no nuance, or of the

139

fluffy 'do-gooder' kind that offers plenty of nice words but *no* clear direction. Either way it will have a dramatically negative effect on both security prospects and economic prospects. The good news is that upholding democracy guarantees the opposite.

*

The immediate choice between staying or leaving is not particularly important long term. The EU *is* destined to implode at some point. It can however be immensely important for those of us living today. Even when seemingly on their last legs power structures can stumble on for quite some time due to their massively influential web of vested interests. Consequently the choice between staying or leaving is a choice between prolonged and gradually intensified agony or long overdue recalibration and the opportunity of a fresh start.

*

Leaving would entail few big bang moments after the dust has settled. Things would gradually get back, in many respects, to how they were during the early 1990s. Free trade with everyone willing. International co-operation based on the principle of organisational separation ensuring that no single trade facilitator would yet again outsize the intended costume. The friction caused by forced 'togetherness', a highly romantic notion indeed, would be abandoned. International relations beyond trade would instead be based on the notion of live and let live as well as ad hoc cooperation when the need and desire is mutual.

*

When things are back in reasonable order and growth curves yet again point steadily upwards, new grandiose political top table schemes will probably be presented, attached with promises of superior solutions to the problems of the day. Hopefully the EU experiment will then serve as a warning example.

*

There is a major difference between internationalism and an international outlook. Forcing everyone into the same shoe is manifestly the mark of *internationalism* but is has never been a truly *international* way of relating to other countries. The former craves an unwavering belief that one political roadmap – which just happens to be your own - is superior to all others. It also craves the power to enforce it. The latter only craves the live and let live attitude, coupled with the realistic view that nothing else will ever work as intended.

*

Now as always back to basics is the best motto to live by if wanting to boost both living standards and peace prospects, meaning *no* experimentation with democracy and beyond that solid legwork. Now as always the greatest challenge is to withstand the do-gooder romantics and smooth-talkers promising delivery through grand schemes.

*

Not in 500 years have political megaprojects had a long shelf-life in Europe. This has been a key element of Europe's remarkable prosperity. Neither will the current one. In fact, the truly European way is to quite quickly abandon political experiments such as the EU.

James B. Buchanan and Gordon Tullock when wrapping up, The Calculus of Consent, the book that triggered the public choice school of thought (p 306)

"We are convinced that man can organize his political society better by putting checkreins on his behavior in advance, checkreins which effectively restrain the behavior of the deviant from the "moral way"— behavior that may be observed only occasionally and temporarily but which may also be quite characteristic of real world human beings... With the philosophers of the Enlightenment we share the faith that man can rationally organize his own society, that existing organization can always be perfected, and that nothing in the social order should remain exempt from rational, critical, and intelligent discussion. Man's reason is the slave to his passions, and recognizing this about himself, man can organize his own association with his fellows in such a manner that the mutual benefits from social interdependence can be effectively maximized."

Selected Bibliography

Concise Encyclopedia of Economics, 2nd edition (2007), online at Econlib

Encyclopædia Britannica Online (2010 edition), Encyclopædia Britannica Inc

The Elgar companion to public choice (2014, 2nd edition), anthology with 43 scholars contributing, edited by Michael Reksulak, Laura Razzolini and William F. Shughart II, Edward Elgar Publishing

The Elgar companion to public choice (2003, 1st edition), anthology with 36 scholars contributing, edited by William F. Shughart II and Laura Razzolini, Edward Elgar Publishing

Daron Acemoglu & James A. Robinson (2013), *Why Nations Fail: The Origins of Power Prosperity and Poverty*, Profile Books

Richard Aldous (2007), *The Lion and the Unicorn: Gladstone vs Disraeli*, Pimlico

Henrietta Barnett and Samuel Barnett (1888), *Practicable Socialism: Essays on Social Reform*, London: Longmans Green and Co

Peter Bernholz and Roland Vaubel (2007), *Political Competition and Economic Regulation*, Routledge (anthology: Bernholz and Vaubel contributors and editors)

Roger Bootle (2015) *The Trouble with Europe* (2nd edition) London: Nicholas Brealey Publishing

Nancy Boyd (1982), *Josephine Butler, Octavia Hill, Florence Nightingale*, The Macmillan Press Ltd

James M. Buchanan and Gordon Tullock (1962), *The Calculus of Consent*, The University of Michigan Press

Rondo Cameron and Larry Neal (2002), *A Concise Economic History of the World: From Paleolithic Times to the Present* (4th Edition), Oxford University Press

Michelle Cini (2007), *From integration to integrity: Administrative ethics and reform in the European Commission*, Manchester University Press

Birte Cordes and Ronald Köhler (2014), *Let's explore Europe!*, European Commission Directorate-General for Communication

Hugo Dixon (2014), *The In/Out Question: Why Britain should stay in the EU*, CreateSpace

Derrida and Habermas (2003) *February 15, or What Binds Europeans Together: A Plea for a Common Foreign Policy, Beginning in the Core of Europe* Blackwell Publishing

Michael Emerson and Karel Lannoo (2015), *Britain's Future in Europe: Reform, renegotiation, repatriation or secession?*, Centre for European Policy Studies

Niall Ferguson (2009), *The Ascent of money: A financial history of the world*, Penguin books

David G. Green (2013), *What have we done: The surrender of our democracy to the EU*, Civitas

David G. Green (2014), *The Demise of the Free State: Why British democracy and the EU don't mix*, Civitas

Jonathan Haidt (2012), *The Righteous Mind: Why Good People are Divided by Politics and Religion*, Allen Lane

Simon Hix and Bjorn Hoyland (2008), The Political System of the European Union, Palgrave Macmillan

Manfred J Holler and Bengt-Arne Wickström (1999), The Scandal Matrix: The Use of Scandals in the Progress of Society. Homo Oeconomicus, Vol. 16

Immanuel Kant (1939) *Perpetual Peace*, Columbia University Press

John Maynard Keynes (1919), *The Economic Consequences of the Peace*, London: Macmillan

Henry Kissinger (2012), *Diplomacy*, Simon & Schuster

Roger Liddle (2014) The Europe Dilemma: Britain and the Drama of EU integration, Policy network

John Locke (2003), *Locke: Political Writings*, Hackett Publishing Company

John McCormick, Understanding the European Union (2011 5th edition), Palgrave Macmillan

Patrick Minford and Vidya Mahambare and Eric Nowell (2005), *Should Britain Leave the EU: An Economic Analysis of a Troubled Relationship*, Edward Elgar with the Institute of Economic Affairs

Charles de Secondat Montesquieu (1990), *Montesquieu: Selected Political Writings*, Hackett Publishing Company

William A. Niskanen (1998), *Policy Analysis and Public Choice*, Edward Elgar publishing

Richard A E North with Robert Oulds (2016), *Flexcit: The Market Solution to leaving the EU* , Bruges Group

Mancur Olson (1965), *The Logic of collective action*, Harvard University Press

Mancur Olson (1982), *The Rise and Decline of Nations*, Yale University Press

Melanie Phillips (2008), *The Ascent of Woman*, Abacus

Gwyn Prins and Johanna Moehring (2008), *Another Europe*, Lilliput

Lee Rotherham (2012) *The EU in a Nutshell: Everything you wanted to know about the European Union but didn't know how to ask* Hampshire: Harriman House

Jan Smuts, (1918), *The League of Nations: A Practical Suggestion*, Hodder and Stoughton

David O. Stewart (2015), *Madison's Gift: Five Partnerships That Built America*, Simon & Schuster

Gert Tinggaard Svendsen (2008), *Lobbyisme i EU*, Forlaget Samfundslitteratur

Loukas Tsoukalis (2014) *The Unhappy State of the Union: Europe needs a new grand bargain*, Policy Network (pamphlet published in partnership with 5 other European think tanks)

Gordon Tullock (1998), *Autocracy*, Kluwer Academic publishers

Roland Vaubel (2009), *The European Institutions as an Interest Group: The Dynamics of Ever-Closer Union*, Institute of Economic Affairs

Roland Vaubel and Thomas D. Willett (1991), *The political economy of international organizations: A public choice approach*, Westview Press (anthology: Vaubel and Willett contributors and editors)

Hugo Young (1999), *This blessed plot: Britain and Europe from Churchill to Blair*, Macmillan

Introduction

[1] The public choice school of thought does indeed stress that the operators of a political system, public servants, do not belong to a species less self-serving than anybody else. Public choice pioneer James Buchanan defined public choice as "politics without romance". Perhaps unsurprisingly the public choice perspective is anathema to many public servants and merely treated as a much disputed 'theory'. This is turn means it typically ranks far down on the priority list when academic budgets are decided; except possibly in a misrepresented form for the sake of appearance.

[2] Jonathan Haidt (2012), *The Righteous Mind: Why Good People are Divided by Politics and Religion* (*p 71*), Allen Lane

[3] Roger Bootle (2015), *The Trouble with Europe*(2nd edition) London: Nicholas Brealey Publishing

[4] Roland Vaubel (2009), *The European Institutions as an Interest Group: The Dynamics of Ever-Closer Union*, Institute of Economic Affairs

[5] David G. Green (2013), *What have we done: The surrender of our democracy to the EU* London: Civitas

[6] The term people has in practice never signified more than a sizeable group of people; every major political system, not least the most despotic, have always been underpinned by a large number of economic dependents.

[7] Jonathan Haidt (2012), *The Righteous Mind: Why Good People are Divided by Politics and Religion* (*p 71*), Allen Lane

Chapter 1

[8] It was only at this time that the strong political influence of the farming collective began to be unique to France. In most other countries the farming collective lost political clout due to both mechanisation and large-scale production. In France these factors made, in relative terms, less of an impact because of the special characteristics of (French) viticulture. In combination

with the continuation of a high level of state/EU subsidies the number of farmers (and their voting strength) has not fallen to the same extent as in most other industrialised countries.

[9] Roger Bootle (2015) *The Trouble with Europe*(2nd edition) London: Nicholas Brealey Publishing

[10] In 1960 the French left French Equatorial Africa and French West Africa; in 1962 they were forced out of Algeria. In 1954 they had also been forced out of French Indochina (Vietnam) and in 1956 Morocco. No conflict was as controversial in France as the Algerian conflict. Many Frenchmen regarded the former general Charles de Gaulle as a traitor after pulling French troops out of Algeria. Thereby he 'abandoned' the section of the Algerian population of European origin (approximately 10 percent of the population).

[11] David G. Green (2013) *What have we done*: *The surrender of our democracy to the EU* London: Civitas

[12] Roland Vaubel, The Elgar companion to public choice (2014), p 464, Edward Elgar Publishing

[13] After the first Danish referendum, held in June 1992, currency problems had crept up the agenda. This was a result of turbulence on the currency markets in September 1992 when Britain was forced to withdraw from the European Exchange Rate Mechanism (ERM). The Swedish krona was also 'broken' but Sweden was not yet in the EU and consequently not formally linked to the ERM.

[14] Schengen has since been extended to include all EU countries except Britain and Ireland. It also includes all four EFTA countries (Norway, Switzerland, Lichtenstein and Iceland).

[15] Large countries lost their extra place on the Commission but were allowed to retain considerably more votes on the council than small countries. In proportion to their populations the small countries received considerably more votes than the larger countries. France refused to accept a smaller weighted vote than Germany, which resulted in Germany, France, Britain and Italy getting 29

votes each, whilst, for instance, Sweden got 10 and Denmark and Finland seven. Germany did however get most seats in the Parliament (99); France, Britain and Italy had 72 each, while Sweden had 18 and Denmark and Finland 13 each.

[16] Whilst 'constitution' normally comprises a framework for the creation of a state, the term 'treaty' usually associated with an agreement between individual sovereign states.

Chapter 2

[17] Pioneers included liberal MPs Richard Cobden and John Bright who famously fought to repeal the Corn Laws.

[18] In the UK part of the UK male working class was given the vote during the latter half of the 19th century; in urban areas (boroughs) in1867 and on the countryside (counties) in 1884.

[19] The notion that hereditary traits determine human qualities was of course, in turn, a fundamental notion underpinning the aristocratic system. Consequently it was challenged even more strongly by the radical left than by the progressives.

[20] It follows that the internationalist model of thought is highly eclectic. As early as in the 17th century thinkers such as Immanuel Kant and Thomas Paine argued that a high degree of rationality could be expected from leaders in republican (democratic) societies. During the consecutive century Liberals such as John Bright and Richard Cobden were instrumental in adding a trading context. Many leftish thinkers, not least those connected with the progressive/socialist Fabian Society, echoed Rousseau when emphasising the importance of the environment and also arguing that experts (social scientists) should play a key role in society planning.

[21] Jürgen Habermas, the German sociologist and philosopher who is the perhaps most influential academic attached to the so called Frankfurt School (the in turn probably most influential social science strand of thought in Europe), has famously built an academic theory, communicative rationality, which is so closely related to the internationalist thought model that it can be considered a modern variety.

[22] The Economist, *Are Eurocrats in it for the money?*, June 22 2010

[23] The Guardian, *Departing MEPs get final payoff of up to £157,000*, April 27 2014

[24] Roger Bootle (2015) *The Trouble with Europe* (2nd edition) London: Nicholas Brealey Publishing

[25] FT June 30 2015

[26] London School of Economics, February14 2014

[27] In the foreword to the *General report on the activities in the European Union 2014*

[28] Roland Vaubel (2007), *Political Competition and Economic Regulation*, Routledge (pp 148-151)

[29] Roland Vaubel, *The Elgar companion to public choice* (2014), pp 455-456, Edward Elgar Publishing

[30] Office for national statistics, quarterly report May 2015

[31] Office for national statistics, Long-Term International Migration Estimates, Frequently Asked Questions and Background Notes, May 2015

[32] A term possibly coined by British writer James Bartholomew in a Spectator article, *Hating the Daily Mail is a substitute for doing good*, April 18 2015

[33] The Guardian, *EU governments push through divisive deal to share 120,000 refugees*, September 22 2015

[34] EU Budget Financial Report 2013, European Commission

[35] Another 50 examples of EU waste, 2010, Open Europe Briefing note

[36] EU Budget Financial Report 2013, European Commission

[37] www.iro.ie/EU-structural-funds.html

[38] Pawel Swidlicki, Raoul Ruparel, Mats Persson, Chris Howarth (2012) *OFF TARGET: The case for bringing regional policy back home*, Open Europe report

[39] EU Budget Financial Report 2013, European Commission

[40] Gert Tinggaard Svendsen (2008), *Lobbyisme i EU* (*p 120-125*), Forlaget Samfundslitteratur

[41] Another 50 examples of EU waste, 2010, Open Europe Briefing note

[42] The Daily Telegraph, *The EU budget is a disaster that cannot save Greece*, August 28 2013.

[43] Panorama magazine Winter 2013 no 48 s 4 *Cohesion Policy 2014-2020 Momentum Builds*, Publications office of the European Union

[44] www.wellspent.eu

[45] Source: EU Budget Financial Report 2014, European Commission

[46] Michel C. Munger, The Elgar companion to public choice (2014), p 53, Edward Elgar Publishing

[47] Roland Vaubel, ibid, p 467

[48] ibid, p 463

[49] European Commission (press release), Commission unveils first EU Anti-Corruption report, February 3 2014

[50] EUObserver, *EU-wide corruption report drops chapter on EU institutions*, January 13 2014

[51] EUObserver, *Commission dismisses Marta Andreasen*, October 13 2004

[52] The Daily Telegraph, *Kinnock EU whistleblower 'hung out to dry'*, July 21 2002

[53] The Guardian, *Europe is out to get me*, January 11 1999

[54] Michelle Cini (2007), *From integration to integrity: Administrative ethics and reform in the European Commission (pp81-107)*, Manchester University Press

[55] The Daily Telegraph, *Euro-court outlaws criticism of EU*, March 7 2001

[56] Financial Times, *Commission worker rebels against judgment of mental instability*, September 15 2006

[57] Mail&Guardian, *Brussels reporter loses battle to protect sources*, April 23 2005

[58] New York Times, *German reporter wins press freedom case in European Court of Human Rights*, November 28 2007

[59] Manfred J Holler and Bengt-Arne Wickström (1999), The Scandal Matrix: The Use of Scandals in the Progress of Society. Homo Oeconomicus, Vol. 16, p 10

[60] Derrida and Habermas (2003), *February 15, or What Binds Europeans Together: A Plea for a Common Foreign Policy, Beginning in the Core of Europe*, Blackwell Publishing

[61] Roland Vaubel (2009), *The European Institutions as an Interest Group: The Dynamics of Ever-Closer Union*, Institute of Economic Affairs

[62] Patrick Minford and Vidya Mahambare and Eric Nowell (2005), *Should Britain Leave the EU: An Economic Analysis of a Troubled Relationship*, Edward Elgar with the Institute of Economic Affairs

[63] Patrick Minford gained prominence after defending the controversial economic policies of the first Thatcher government after these had been publicly challenged by 364 leading economists.

[64] Speech titled "Reforming Europe in a changing world", available to watch at the European Commission website

[65] Euronews, *Nobel winner Jean Tirole speaks out in favour of a European budget*, October 17 2015

[66] New York Times, *Ending Greece's Nightmare*, January 26 2015

[67] The Guardian, *How I would vote in the Greek referendum*, June 29 2015

[68] Dagens Nyheter, *Cameron's EU populism will hurt Sweden*, May 17 2015. One article of thousands which includes a line of reasoning that arguably provides a good illustration of the thought pattern 'accepted' in Swedish media: "The EU is a peace project, it is undoubtedly beneficial and empowering to be a member, David Cameron's call for a referendum was opportunistic and unnecessarily prompted by a small group of conspiring Thatcherite nationalists. There is nothing seriously wrong with the EU. It should actually be considered as the injured party while a handy scapegoat for domestic member state problems. There is a link between racists and those seeking member state power repatriation." This particular article written by the political editor of the largest morning paper. The same editor has also been – and remains - one of the staunchest supporters of the controversial open border experiment briefly attempted by the Swedish government during late 2015.

Chapter 3

[69] Rondo Cameron and Larry Neal (2002), *A Concise Economic History of the World: From Paleolithic Times to the Present* (4th Edition), Oxford University Press

[70] Erasmus is an EU funded university exchange student *and* staff training programme which was created by the EU in 1987 with the purpose of bring

Europeans closer together. By 2013 three million Europeans had been Erasmus students and the number of institutions for higher education taking part amounted to 3,200. Source: EU commission report (2013), *Supporting reform: The role of Erasmus in higher education*, Luxembourg publications office of the European Union.

[71] A landmark study concerning rent-seeking produced by Mancur Olson (1965), *The Logic of collective action*, Harvard University Press

[72] The public choice term for quid pro quo support is logrolling and refers back to an old timber industry practice when neighbours helped each other to move logs.

[73] In the foreword to the *General report on the activities in the European Union 2014*

Chapter 4

[74] The argument is well presented by Hugo Dixon in his book *The In/Out Question: Why Britain should stay in the EU*.

[75] http://europa.eu/europedirect/meet_us/unitedkingdom/index_en.htm

[76] http://europa.eu/europedirect/meet_us/unitedkingdom/index_en.htm

[77] Cambridge dictionary online

[78] europa.eu/teachers-corner

[79] www.gov.uk/government/speeches/eu-speech-at-bloomberg (Jan 23, 2013)

[80] The Guardian, *David Cameron's EU deal: What he wanted and what he got*, Feb 19 2016

[81] The Telegraph, *EU deal: What David Cameron asked for... and what he actually got*, Feb 20 2016

[82] The Times, *In or out? European referendum set for June 23*, Feb 20 2016

Chapter 5

[83] *Why the Government believes that voting to remain in the European Union is the best decision for the UK*, EU referendum leaflet produced by the UK government and distributed to UK households on April 11 2016

[84] As it happens there is an international mobile operator association, GSMA,

with a global rather than only European reach, headquartered in London.

[85] Richard A E North with Robert Oulds (2016), *Flexcit: The Market Solution to leaving the EU* , Bruges Group

[86] Where next? A liberal, free-market guide to Brexit (April 2016), Open Europe report

Printed in Poland
by Amazon Fulfillment
Poland Sp. z o.o., Wrocław